The Coming Collapse of the American Republic

And What You Can Do To Prevent It

Robert A. Hall

All author's proceeds from this book will be donated to
a charity to help wounded troops and their families

Copyright © Robert A. Hall, 2011
Old Jarhead Publishing
Des Plaines, IL
All rights reserved
ISBN-13: 978-1461122531
ISBN-10: 1461122538
Library of Congress Control Number: 2011906684

Dedication

To all Marines, past, present and future, but especially to Col. John Studt, USMC (Ret.), my Commanding Officer in the 25th Marines and the best officer I served under, to the late Maj. Gene Duncan (Ret.), a Marine icon I was proud to call my friend, and to my Drill Instructors from Parris Island Platoon 273, 1964, Sergeants William H. Harris, Michael P. Martin and Ezekiel Owens, Jr., who gave me the discipline to have a wonderful life. It was the privilege of a lifetime to wear the same uniform as all of you, and I have tried every day to re-earn the right to be among your ranks, even if standing at the rear.

Royalties

The author has directed that all his profits from this book be given to the Injured Marine Semper Fi Fund (www.semperfifund.org), which is a nonprofit set up to provide immediate financial support for injured members of U.S. Armed Forces and their families. They direct urgently needed resources to Marines and Sailors, as well as members of the Army, Air Force or Coast Guard who serve in support of Marine forces. Checks may be sent to the Injured Marine Semper Fi Fund, 825 College Blvd, Suite 102, PMB 609, Oceanside, CA 92057. This book is, however, not endorsed or supported by the Semper Fi Fund, and in fact they had no advance knowledge the author was going to write it or to direct the royalties to their cause. The author is solely to blame for it, including for opinions and for any errors, or for sleepless nights it may cause you. Should the Semper Fi Fund not be accepting donations, the funds will go to another veterans' charity, not to the author.

Acknowledgements

Special thanks go to Bonnie Hall, my wife, cheerleader and tireless proofreader, to Chet Nagle, a naval aviator, experienced intelligence operative and author who offered professional editing and a critique, to my Marine comrades Ron "Count" Pittenger and R. J. Del Vecchio for diligent proofreading and comment, and to Thomas J. Hall, a very knowledgeable intellectual property attorney who volunteered to check the quotations to be sure they were within the bounds of "Fair Use," and kindly offered additional editorial input. Tom, who is co-author of the well-received *Application Service Provider and Software as a Service Agreements Line by Line*, wishes it known that his last name is a coincidence, that he is not a relative and is not responsible for any errors in this work. Nor are my other volunteer editors. Without the diligent efforts of these individuals to eliminate many of my typos and sloppy usage, this work would have been far poorer.

About the Author

Robert A. Hall has been a successful non-profit executive since 1982. Prior to entering that field, Hall served five terms in the Massachusetts State Senate. He was first elected in 1972, the year he graduated from college, defeating a Democrat incumbent by nine votes out of 60,000 cast, in a 4-1 Democrat district, last won by a Republican in 1938. He was re-elected four times by increasing margins, carrying every city and town in the district, and was nominated by both parties in 1976. He was Minority Whip when he retired undefeated in 1982.

Hall holds an Associate's degree in liberal arts from Mount Wachusett Community College (1970), a Bachelor's degree in government from the University of Massachusetts (1972) and a Master's of Education degree in history from Fitchburg State University (1980).

He is also a Marine Vietnam veteran, having served four years in the regulars before college and, while a senator, another six in the reserves, finishing with the rank of Staff Sergeant.

A frequently-published freelance writer, Hall's columns, articles, short stories and poetry have appeared in over 75 local and national publications. His book of anecdotes about the Marines and politics, *The Good Bits*, was published by www.authorhouse.com in 2005. His book on association management, *Chaos for Breakfast: Practical Help and Humor for the Non-profit Executive* was published in 2008 by the American Society of Association Executives, www.asaecenter.org. (Royalties go to charity.) *CYA: Protecting Yourself in the Modern Jungle*, a humor/self-help book was produced by PublishAmerica in 2010. www.publishamerica.net/product93291.html

He has been married to his first wife, Bonnie, since 1992. Currently he manages an association, reads extensively and writes articles for his political blog, *The Old Jarhead*. (www.tartanmarine.blogspot/com). He is a former Scottish Country Dancer, but has Pulmonary Fibrosis, an eventually-terminal illness that curtails his physical activities as he requires oxygen for mobility. Comments, fan letters and hate mail, which he enjoys sharing, may be sent to him at tartanmarine@gmail.com.

Contents:

Introduction: Will There Be a Collapse?

The world probably needs another, "The End is Coming" book like it needs another Ice Age. That, you will recall, was one of the big scares of the 1970s, generating lots of ink, making money for some people, and not only wasn't it remotely true, the last decade has featured "Global Warming" as the scare du jour, getting lots of ink and making money for some people. Quite a lot of money, in many cases.

The other big scare of the Seventies was *The Population Bomb*, by Paul Ehrlich. My professors presented it to me as *settled science* along with its apocalyptic vision of world wide famine and the end of civilization due to the depletion of all strategic minerals. That didn't happen, either, but it factored into my decision to remain single until I was 46 and to not have progeny of my own (my granddaughter is by marriage). Given the collapsing birthrate in the civilized countries, my decision may have contributed to the coming fall, but more about that later.

And neither the Alor on red apples nor Agent Orange from Vietnam has killed me—yet. My IPF is not from Agent Orange, but probably from my mother, who died of it, much as I might like to stick the taxpayers with the bill and get some bragging right for having been killed by my service in Vietnam.

I should have learned from all this that predicting disaster is an activity fraught with egg-on-the-face. Nor does the soothsayer who predicts mostly bad things get much repeat business at the fair. As Mark Twain said, "I have lived a long life and had many troubles, most of which never happened."

The adage in the news business is that, "Good News is No News." And yet, as I compiled items of interest for my political blog, *The Old Jarhead*, I saw trends that portend desperate challenges for our nation. Since the US is still, in Lincoln's timeless phrase, "The last, best hope of mankind," folks in the rest of the civilized world will have little time to enjoy their *schadenfreude* if disaster comes to this Republic, no matter their feelings towards us.

My concerns led me to write an essay with the same title as this book, which I published on my blog in March of 2010, and sent to my mailing list. At 4,200 words, it was too long for publication in the traditional mainstream media or even on most commercial blogs, given the attention span of the reading public.

But still it nagged at me, as the news grew more alarming. The current state of my health suggests this is not a personal problem, but I have a granddaughter I love, and I care about the future of not only her and the children of friends and relatives, but of freedom, civilization and all the children to come. This slim book is my attempt to reach a larger audience, not for personal gain, but so I can feel that I went down fighting.

So, will there be a Collapse?

This is not an anti-Obama book, though I'm certainly not an Obama supporter. I do not think that the country is going to collapse because Barack

Obama was elected. I do think that President Obama's naiveté, incompetence, statist political orientation and political debts to public unions and big spenders have accelerated the problem, and will continue to do so. But there is enough blame for both parties and all citizens—yes, including me. We have all failed, in greater or lesser part, to preserve this "City on a Hill."

The United States was a great country while it lasted. But nothing tangible lasts forever, not stars, nor planets, nor people nor flowers nor butterflies. Certainly not political systems. We can be certain that the American Republic will have an ending as surely as it had a beginning. But will it be in the lifetime of many now alive?

Predicting the future is not an easy task—otherwise, I'd spend more time at the racetrack. In the hundreds of opinion pieces I've published over the years, I've had some notable success doing so. In 1998, three years before 9/11, I published a column about the War on Terror in which I wrote that terrorists now had the power to destroy large buildings. Prescient, perhaps, but I've made my share of predictions that were embarrassingly off the mark.

Emerging trends or sudden events can completely alter what looked to be inevitable. The death of a key leader, a new technology, a natural disaster striking your country—or your opponent's—these and other unforeseeable events can alter the seemingly-inevitable future. We may certainly hope for a "Game Changer" that will make this book so much drivel. Nothing would please me more. History gives us hope. "The Great Horse Manure Crisis of 1894" was resolved by the invention of the automobile—bringing new challenges.[1]

Certainly the American Republic has been both resilient and flexible since its improbable emergence from the fire of revolution. It survived a terrible civil war, an outcome that seemed highly unlikely at the time. It survived the Great Depression, despite the best efforts of our leaders to prolong it.[2] It led and won the fight against global tyranny in WWII, a victory that may appear inevitable now, but was a damn close thing at the time. And it faced down the monster of soulless Communism, despite the infatuation of large numbers of our vapid intellectual class with the joys of collectivism, as seen from afar and applied to others.

And yet, despite this history of resilience and triumph, I think that there is about an 80% likelihood that the American Republic will collapse within the next twenty years, and be replaced with something else—perhaps several independent jurisdictions. It certainly is being changed far beyond what the Founders would have recognized as a Republic. If so, it is certain that what emerges will not be a model of classical liberal democracy. That this collapse will be characterized by economic privation, great violence, mass suffering and extensive death I consider inevitable. That the surviving citizens of the new entity or entities will enjoy anything close to our freedom or standard of living I believe highly unlikely. The Jamestown rule—no work, no eat—will be rigidly enforced. Many of today's highly-compensated skills will be almost worthless (including mine), but things like hunting, farming and basic nursing will be prized. The old and sick who require a lot of resources and are not able to contribute physically—such as those of us dependent on bottled oxygen—will be, of necessity, tossed out of the lifeboats.

Each of the several challenges facing us is both complex and over-whelming, and we no longer seem to have "the right stuff" to deal with any of them. While we might successfully, though not painlessly, face down each of them individually, their convergence makes the Republic's survival highly problematic. Americans want the benefits of the good life, but far too many want someone else to pay the costs and make the sacrifices for them to have it. Few are willing to sacrifice their comfort, their cash or their standard of living—never mind their lives—to protect the Republic and the system of political and economic freedom and property rights that created the American material wealth that is the envy of the planet, far beyond what our grandfathers could have dreamed. Just one example: In WWII, our forces were led by graduates of Harvard, Yale and other leading institutions. Since Vietnam, military services is disparaged and shunned by the elites who benefit the most from our system. ROTC is banned at the Ivies, on one pretext or another. Takers far outnumber givers.

Edward Gibbon wrote, "In the end more than they wanted freedom, they wanted security. When the Athenians finally wanted not to give to society but for society to give to them, when the freedom they wished for was freedom from responsibility, then Athens ceased to be free." It is hard to dispassionately observe the United States, or most of what I call the civilized world, without seeing his words reflected in the views and behavior of a majority of citizens.

We are victims of our economic success. Fat and comfortable Republics have ever been prey to wolves and barbarians, and, in our case, there are perhaps as many inside the gates as outside.

This book focuses on the four convergent forces that I believe are likely to destroy the Republic, not that there are not additional problems which will complicate our responses.

Chapter One: The Federal Government is Broke. Really.

A friend of mine once said, loosely translated for a family audience, "Bob, it's money and women makes the world go round. And if you've got one, you can get the other." Well, the fair sex with all its power of attraction is still thankfully with us, but there is no longer any money to get.

Lobbyists and politicians fighting in Washington for an ever-bigger slice of the pie for clients and constituents are fighting over a crust that covers a pie tin filled with IOUs. They resemble nothing so much as the Nazi hierarchy still jockeying for political position with the Fuhrer in March of 1945, as the Soviet and Allied armies closed in to put a just end to their world forever.

For years, everyone who was paying attention at all has known that a fiscal disaster was looming. And we fretted about it. The problem was so huge that we mostly averted our eyes and hoped someone else would fix it. Like the threat of a large meteor-strike or a super-eruption of a volcano, we hoped its seeming inevitability would happen, if at all, long after our children's grandchildren had passed from the stage.

That is not to be. The financial catastrophe is now so close that even the first wave of the baby boomer generation will suffer, absent the escape of an early demise. Public debt far beyond our means to pay is the rule at every level of government. And it is not just the United States that is in bad shape—not even the worst shape—but all the developed countries.

Government insolvency has, of course been a consistent feature of the third world, requiring frequent rescues by the developed countries in a cycle of loans and loan forgiveness. That these efforts have failed to benefit many citizens beyond the local blood-soaked oligarchy has been known to all paying attention, and ignored by almost everyone, in hopes that bread and circuses will keep the mob at bay. When they discover that there will be no more rescues—the life preservers are gone—things will get mean.

In his *Newsweek* article, "The West and the Tyranny of Public Debt,"[1] Jacques Attali writes, "But never, outside periods of total war, has the debt of the world's most powerful states grown so immense. Never has it so heavily threatened their political systems and standards of living. Public debt cannot keep growing without unleashing terrible catastrophes. Anyone saying this today is accused of pessimism."

I highly recommend you stop reading now, go to your computer, and locate this article, which provides the historic context needed to grasp the enormity of the coming tragedy.

(http://www.newsweek.com/2010/12/27/the-west-and-the-tyranny-of-public-debt.html)

Ah, you're back. You look a tad pale and shaky, but let's proceed.

Not a week goes by that I don't post a link to a story of government fiscal desperation on my blog. But each of these articles focuses on one problem, in one area. Let's take a brief tour of the mind-numbing problem and try to tie these frightening pieces together. Please be thinking of solutions, as there will be a quiz. If you are under, say, 55 and healthy, your standard of living and perhaps your life will depend on there being solutions.

The United States Government

We'll start at the top, with the problem that everyone is familiar with. Or, perhaps, familiar with part of—the federal deficit. Writing about this is difficult. Almost every day brings in new information. I'm writing early in 2011. By the time this gets in print, the numbers I include will be badly outdated. And the situation will be far worse; is in fact growing worse at a rate that is hard to grasp.

As I write, the federal deficit is ... well, I don't really know the size of the true deficit, if you count all the obligations the US Government is definitely or likely on the hook for. I'm not sure anyone does. But here are some of the most important parts of the puzzle.

The Federal Deficit

According to the Mercatus Center at George Washington University, "The U.S. national debt currently stands at 62 percent of GDP—its highest level since WWII. Under plausible assumptions, this ratio will rise to at least 80 percent and possibly 185 percent of GDP by 2035 and continue increasing thereafter. As the debt ratio increases, the country's creditors will demand higher and higher interest rates to continue financing this debt. This means even larger deficits and ultimately a U.S. default. Both macroeconomic and microeconomic perspectives suggest that tax increases cannot address the debt problem because higher taxes mean slower economic growth, reducing the scope for increased tax revenue."[2]

These numbers are meaningless, of course, to most folks. In fact, most folks aren't paying attention at all—more on that later. But even to those who are, is this so bad? Especially as so many of the EU countries, especially the PIIGS (Portugal, Ireland, Italy, Greece and Spain) are far worse off. According to an article in the *Washington Post* in March, 2010, "Greece's national debt last year reached 113 percent of gross domestic product. The United States will hit that in about 2020, according to the Government Accountability Office, assuming policy continues as it has. And last year's U.S. budget deficit amounted to 9.9 percent of GDP, nearly rivaling Greece's 12.7 percent."[3] The columnist is not considered a conservative.

Nor is Greece an anomaly. In April of 2010, the *Irish Central* reported, "It has been confirmed that Ireland has the highest national debt in Europe. Ireland has a deficit of 14.3 percent of its gross domestic product (GDP) and has surpassed Greece's national debt, which is 13.6% of its GDP."[4]

We should take small comfort in Europe's problems, any more than a man who is to be hanged next Tuesday feels relieved because his cellmate is to be executed in the morning. Besides, as 2008 showed with the worldwide banking collapse, and in fact 1933 showed with the Smoot-Hawley-driven world trade collapse that locked in the Great Depression, the world's economy is so integrated that pain quickly spreads through the global economic system like an aggressive infection.

Reuters reports that the Congressional Budget Office estimates, "The U.S. debt will top $13.6 trillion this year (in 2010) and climb to an estimated $19.6 trillion by 2015, according to a Treasury Department report to Congress. The report that was sent to lawmakers Friday night with no fanfare said the ratio of debt to the gross domestic product would rise to 102 percent by 2015 from 93 percent this year."[5]

Not only are the numbers so huge as to be hard to grasp for the average person—that includes me and probably you—but as you will have noted above, there are wide variations in the "hugeness" of the numbers. This may be a case of, "figures don't lie, but liars figure." More likely it reflects the variations in projections that individuals are likely to make, depending on their competence and political orientation, and on what they include or exclude from the projected deficit. You will remember when supportive Congressmen, not that long ago, were saying that Fannie Mae and Freddie Mac were not only sound, but would never cost the taxpayers a nickel, as only the investors were at risk. If only that had been true. Do these deficit projections include future liabilities for Fannie and Freddie? What else will the taxpayers have to cover? Who knows without digging into the costs with our own accounting team?

What we do know is that the deficit has increased at an unbelievable rate since 2007, dwarfing all previous government debts—and giving rise to the Tea Party, as it frightened those who were paying attention.

Every dollar that government spends must be taxed from the private sector, or borrowed, thus reducing money available for private sector economic development while increasing the debt, or printed, creating an inflationary tax on everyone.

What happens when no one will lend us more money? Moody's says the US is in danger of losing its AAA bond rating. Such a downgrade would, of course, cost additional billions of dollars annually in increased interest payments on the debt. And at some point, China and everyone else will say, "That's all there is!" Barron's has reported, "China is pulling back from U.S. Treasury securities and buying up hard assets around the world."[6] A pull back by creditors is probably inevitable. After all, we are not the only debtor nation in the world. The EU has put a temporary patch on Greece and Ireland, the canaries in Europe's coal mine, but that will only delay their coming disaster. Just like our leaders, the EU politicians are kicking the can down the road, getting reelected by buying benefits through debt on their watch. But the day is fast approaching when the can won't budge no matter how hard it's kicked.

Faced with a default, the tempting option will be for the US Government, like so many before it, to print money. We are starting to see what they call "quantitative easing," or QE, where, in a second round, the Fed is printing $600 billion to buy back our debt. It is supposed to stimulate the economy, but it does so by making all of our savings worth less. "The Chinese ratings agency, Dagong, scorned QE as 'a practice resembling drinking poison to quench thirst... In essence the depreciation of the US dollar adopted by the US government indicates that its solvency is on the brink of collapse.'" [7]

Fiat money eventually creates hyper-inflation, as Robert Mugabe could tell Barack Obama, destroying savings and wealth. Money sucked out of the private economy by government reduces economic activity, jobs and, eventually, government revenues, creating a re-enforcing death-spiral.

Dr. Gerald Swanson asked in 1986, "What would life be like in the United States with an inflation rate of 20% or more? South America offers a number of clues. At one time in Argentina, a pair of shoes cost as much as an entire steer. With hyperinflation, prices cannot be used as benchmarks for decisions, since yesterday's prices do not offer any relevancy for today. In fact, it isn't unusual for South American shoppers to see the price of bread increase between the time they enter a grocery store and the time they leave it. Savings lose their value. The only incentive is to spend." [8] Once our government can no longer borrow, we shall find out.

Social Security and Medicare

Everyone's favorite whipping boys, Social Security, Medicare and the Baby Boomers are the public face of the fiscal black hole. In 2009, the National Center for Policy Analysis reported, "The 2009 Social Security and Medicare Trustees Reports show the combined unfunded liability of these two programs has reached nearly $107 trillion in today's dollars! That is about seven times the size of the U.S. economy and 10 times the size of the outstanding national debt." [9] They also estimated that, "By 2030, about the midpoint of the baby boomer retirement years, the programs will require nearly half of all income tax dollars." [9]

These programs are often described as a huge Ponzi scheme, but that probably does Ponzi—and his protégée Bernie Madoff—a disservice, because the scope of the problem is breathtaking. Every dollar that comes in goes to pay for current beneficiaries. The vaunted trust funds for Social Security and Medicare "exist purely for accounting purposes....The accumulated Social Security surplus actually consists of paper certificates (non-negotiable bonds) kept in a filing cabinet in a government office in West Virginia. These bonds cannot be sold on Wall Street or to foreign investors....they are little more than IOUs the government writes to itself." [9] What would the government do to a private company that ran its pension plan in this manner? Would not the executives be headed for prison?

That was in 2009, when Social Security had a $31.7B income surplus. By 2010, that surplus had disappeared, and Social Security was paying out more than it took in. "The annual report of the Social Security Trustees....forecast that the primary Social Security program....would not exceed its tax receipts until 2018. Unfortunately, it happened in fiscal 2010....a whopping $40 billion shortfall."[10] And that was before the first of the Baby Boom Generation (that would include me) turned 65 in 2011. Congress now predicts that Social security will run $600 billion in deficits over the next decade, and will continue to run deficits until the "Trust Fund" is exhausted in 2037.[11] Remember that the "Trust Fund" consists entirely of US Bonds which must be paid back from taxes or borrowing before it can be paid out.

Why is Social Security collapsing? "In 1945, 41.9 workers supported each (Social Security recipient), while today only 3.3 workers support each retiree. That number will continue to shrink."[12] As the Baby Boomers retire, it will shrink ever more rapidly. And with increased life expectancy, the deficit will grow. Social Security Disability has also burgeoned in the recession, as people who can't find work discover they are disabled. It's one of the fastest growing parts of Social Security.

Do you think that the government can raise taxes enough to cover that obligation? For how long? In 2050, these programs will consume almost all current tax revenues.[8] Liberals and conservatives can debate at what point higher taxes drive jobs and productive individuals out of the economy, but at some point the goose dies and you get no more golden eggs to buy votes. I think few economists would say that tax increases gigantic enough to meet the unfunded liability would not have a very negative impact on the economy, costing millions of jobs and driving money out of the country. Though given the situation in the rest of the developed world, we may take comfort in the thought that there is almost no safe place to move cash to.

"Tax Day is a dreaded deadline for millions, but for nearly half of U.S. households it's simply somebody else's problem. About 47 percent will pay no federal income taxes at all for 2009."[13] What will be the political ramifications of telling this 47% they have to lose benefits or get back on the tax rolls to cover ever-increasing Social Security and Medicare costs? Or of telling the 53% who still pay federal income taxes that those taxes are going to double? Or triple?

No politician can raise taxes anywhere near enough to meet these obligations and survive politically. (Or maybe even survive, when things get nasty.) Nor can one significantly cut the entitlements and survive. In my area of Cook County Illinois, a challenger suggested raising the Social Security retirement age for younger workers, and the incumbent immediately began running ads with seniors saying, "Keep your hands off the Social Security I worked for, young man!" She lost, but what will happen when the ads are true and about massive Social Security benefit cuts and huge tax hikes to fund what is left?

All of the efforts to date have been short fixes designed to postpone the problem a bit. For example, I cannot draw full Social Security until I reach age 66 in 2011. These types of changes don't fix the problem, they just postpone it. Given my age and health, that may be enough for me. But not for the country.

So we know the National Debt is over $14 trillion and climbing rapidly, and we've added in another $107 trillion for Social Security and Medicare, with Medicare being the largest problem. "Medicare's total unfunded liability is more than five times larger than that of Social Security. In fact, the new

Medicare prescription drug benefit enacted in 2006 (Part D) alone adds some $17 trillion to the projected Medicare shortfall - an amount greater than all of Social Security's unfunded obligations."[9] Thank you George W. Bush.

But is $107 trillion the right number?

One of the ways that the Patient Protection and Affordable Care Act (PPACA—called "Healthcare Reform" by proponents and "Obamacare" by opponents like me) promised to cut the deficit, despite providing broad new entitlements, was by cutting Medicare expenditures by as much as $500 billion per year.

First, it assumed that doctors' Medicare reimbursement fees would be cut. There is a formula called the Sustainable Growth Rate (SGR) that has mandated cuts in physician reimbursement every year. And every year since 2002, the Congress has postponed the cuts with a "patch." There were several short patches in 2010, and the lame duck 111th Congress passed another year long patch postponing what was by then a 23%+ cut for another year—at a projected cost of $17 billion to $20 billion. (Full disclosure—I work for an association that lobbies for a permanent fix to the SGR problem, so I have a bias here.) "Now, the cost of a permanent fix tops $200 billion. The AMA (American Medical Association) made passing a permanent fix its top priority for comprehensive health care reform. But as lawmakers struggled to keep reform's costs under President Barack Obama's $900 billion mark, the enormous price tag of the fix forced lawmakers to exclude it from both the House and Senate bills." [14]

Doctors are already opting out of Medicare. "The number of doctors refusing new Medicare patients because of low government payment rates is setting a new high, just six months before millions of Baby Boomers begin enrolling ..."[15] Medicare patients are already finding it difficult to find care. If the proposed SGR cuts go through, doctors who will begin losing money on Medicare will have no choice but to bail out of the system. Much the same thing is happening with Medicaid at the state level, and the PPACA has just expanded that problem for states in a way few people seem to grasp.

Seniors who are covered but who can't find a doctor to accept the reimbursement rate are in no better shape than the people without coverage in line with them at the emergency room. Yet, even without these cuts, the AMA reports "17% of more than 9,000 doctors surveyed restrict the number of Medicare patients in their practice. Among primary care physicians, the rate is 31%."[13] Who will take care of the 2.8 million baby boomers who join Medicare in 2011, and more each year after that, for the near future? How likely are politicians, who know that angry seniors vote, to actually make the additional cuts to Medicare envisioned in the cost "savings" of ObamaCare? To believe that the PPACA will really reduce the deficit is to believe that politicians will willingly vote themselves out of office.

Medicare, Social Security and the PPACA are the most visible of the federal entitlement programs. But they aren't the only ones.

In FY2006, military retires cost the Federal Government over $40 billion per year and the unfunded liability was $684 billion[16]. Small taters compared to Social Security, perhaps, and certainly owed to those who served. But an added fiscal entitlement none the less.

Then there is the cost of healthcare for both active duty and retired members of our military, about ten million folks. "Total health care costs for the Pentagon, which is the nation's single largest employer, top $50 billion a year, a tenth of its budget and about the same amount that it is spending this year on the war in Iraq. Ten years ago, health care cost the Pentagon $19 billion; five years from now it is projected to cost $65 billion."[17]

Then there's the Veterans Administration, which spends $60 billion a year caring for vets with service connected disabilities, or retirees and other vets in need.[18] (I know a Navy vet, not retired, not service connected, but who needed a lung transplant for IPF, which he received from the VA gratis on the basis of his service. I do not say it wasn't deserved, and I was glad he got it. My survival may soon depend on a similar transplant. But such things are not cheap. How long can we pay for them?)

Getting more attention due to the fiscal crisis are the Civil Service Retirement System (CSRS) and the Federal Employees' Retirement System (FERS). "All assets of the CSRDF (Civil Service Retirement and Disability Fund) are invested in U.S. Treasury bonds and other securities backed by the full faith and credit of the U.S. government. Retirement annuities for federal employee are paid from the CSRDF ... The Office of Personnel Management (OPM) estimates that in FY2010, expenditures from the CSRDF will total $70.2 billion ..."[19] So the retirement system is fully funded—but that fund, like the Social Security Trust Fund, has been borrowed by the U.S. Government to pay current operating expenses and replaced with government IOUs. If I worked for a company with a retirement fund invested solely in that company's bonds, I'd be kind of nervous.

But the government isn't concerned. "Because CSRS retirement benefits have never been fully funded by employer and employee contributions, the Civil Service Retirement and Disability Fund has an unfunded liability. The unfunded liability was $674.2 billion in FY2008. According to actuarial estimates, the unfunded liability of the CSRDF will continue to rise until about 2030, when it will peak at $853.1 billion. From that point onward, the unfunded liability will steadily decline, reaching a projected level of $4.5 billion in the year 2085. Actuarial estimates indicate that the unfunded liability of the CSRS does not pose a threat to the solvency of the trust fund."[18]

As already noted, you also owe money to support Fannie Mae and Freddie Mac, the government supported programs to provide affordable housing to the poor, which conservative economists blame for the start of the economic collapse, by creating the housing bubble. Economist Thomas Sowell, for example, said, "....the risky mortgages had led to huge numbers of defaults, dragging down Fannie Mae, Freddie Mac and the financial markets in general and with them the whole economy."[20]

Remember when Congresswoman Maxine Waters said, "We do not have a crisis at Freddie Mac and particularly Fannie Mae under the outstanding leadership of Frank Raines."[21] Yes, that would be the same Franklin Raines whose legal bills, along with those of other Fannie and Freddie executives, the taxpayers are picking up. But that's only about $160 million you and I owe so far—hardly a blip in this discussion.[22]

How much do you owe for Freddie and Fannie, which supportive politicians promised wouldn't cost you anything? "For all the focus on the historic federal rescue of the banking industry, it is the government's decision to seize Fannie Mae and Freddie Mac in September 2008 that is likely to cost taxpayers the most money. So far the tab stands at $145.9 billion, and it grows with every foreclosure of a three-bedroom home with a two-car garage one hour from Phoenix. The Congressional Budget Office predicts that the final bill could reach $389 billion."[23]

There are other areas where the federal government has made promises and legal commitments, some small, some large. The feds may have to bail out the Post Office. People keep floating plans for the government to bail out public pension plans for cities and states. Digging into all of them could turn this small effort into an encyclopedia. And at this point the numbers are probably meaningless. What is the true total owed? It is probably impossible to know. And if you are now having trouble keeping millions, billions and trillions straight, you aren't alone.

We do know that the current deficit of well over $14 trillion—money the government has spent and owes to folks it borrowed it from, including the trust funds, is dwarfed by the "unfunded liability"—money the government owes by statute, contract or promise in the future, but has not yet spent—and doesn't have.

We certainly know that the situation ranges from very desperate to unavoidably cataclysmic. Unfortunately, I lean toward the "Oh, dear God" end of the range. Certainly, you can do an internet search and find folks offering rays of hope. But to me, they are like the folks on the stern of the Titanic assuring each other that the ship is unsinkable—and it's all dry back here!

Keep in mind there are a number of analysts who think the numbers above are far too optimistic! A *Heritage Foundation* report says, "The new Congressional Budget Office (CBO) 10-year budget baseline shows a virtually unprecedented sea of red ink. ... $1.5 trillion deficit in fiscal year (FY) 2011—an increase of $95 billion over their last 2011 estimate ... This will be the third consecutive year of trillion-dollar deficits. However, the baseline includes a number of unrealistic assumptions—assumptions that Congress requires the CBO to use—that skew the results. Once the baseline is scrubbed of these unrealistic assumptions, the more realistic baseline shows historic spending levels driving the budget deficit to $1.9 trillion by 2021. Over the next decade, deficits are projected to total $13.6 trillion."[24] The report estimates that the per-household debt will increase by $140,000 between 2009 and 2023, so I hope you have a good savings plan to cover your share.

If you think higher taxes are the solution, historically, higher taxes have led to higher spending. A study found that "over the entire post World War II era through 2009 each dollar of new tax revenue was associated with $1.17 of new spending. Politicians spend the money as fast as it comes in—and a little bit more."[25] Besides, "higher taxes mean slower economic growth, reducing the scope for increased tax revenue." [25]

If you want to know how much you and your kids owe, look at the U.S. Debt Clock.[26]

Unfortunately, the fiscal disaster isn't limited to the federal government. The states and local governments are also fiscal wastelands.

Chapter Two: The States are Broke Too.
So are the Cities.

If it were only the government of the United States facing fiscal disaster, we could all ride to the rescue, painful and costly as that would be. It reminds me of my Floor Leader in the Massachusetts Senate, the late Senator John Parker, asking me after what he considered a bad vote on my part, "Bob, where's that big white horse you rode in here on?"

"I had to shoot him and eat him last year, John," I replied.

Our states and cities are eating the horses, and the dogs are worried. Yes, as any student of history can tell you, there have been fiscal troubles before for governments, especially during what used to be called "panics," and now are called "recessions." But not even during the "Great Depression," were the government indebtedness and fiscal problems so deep—or spread so wide.

It's especially hard to get good numbers on the extent of the problem at the state level, or to know which experts to believe. According to WatchDog.org, "Aggregate state debt now exceeds $1.8 trillion, with much more potentially hidden off the official books. The biggest problem-states include Alabama, California, New York, Illinois, Massachusetts, and Pennsylvania." [1] Add that debt to the federal debt of $14 trillion and counting.

Unfortunately, the "biggest problem states" aren't the only problem. Texas is often cited as a state doing well in the recession, through pro-business policies and low taxes. But the "Texas budget is expected to run a $27 billion two-year budget shortfall according to just-released state estimates." [2] Yes, that's still pretty good compared to California, Illinois or New York, but it's not to be celebrated, either.

WatchDog.org goes on to say, "As of 2009, total state debt averages almost $17,000 for each of the 107 million private sector workers in the United States. Pensions and Other Post Employment Benefits play a crucial role in budget strain. Minimum unfunded liabilities totaled more than $1 trillion before markets crashed and states deferred their Annual Required Contributions. Estimates of the true retirement liability are as high as $3 trillion, and Unemployment Trust Fund loans and stagnant employment rates add billions more." [1]

Why are the states and cities in such bad shape? Of course, the recession is a significant factor. But vote-buying by politicians at all levels and in both parties has greatly added to the critical mass. Nothing is more tempting for a politician than to secure the support of a favored group in the next election—just two years away at most—with largess that won't have to be paid for until 15 or 20 years down the road. Unfortunately, we are now "down the road." WatchDog. com cites research by the Mercatus Center that, "since 1950, private spending has increased 5-fold while state and local government spending has increased nearly 10-fold. Real state and local spending growth has consistently outpaced growth in both real GDP and real private GDP. Because state and local governments depend on the private sector for their tax revenue, this path is not sustainable; state and local government spending cannot continually outpace the wealth-creating sector of the economy."[3]

If you search for "state deficits" on the internet, you will find any number of articles and sources—often with conflicting numbers—putting many states billions of dollars in the red. Just raising taxes doesn't cure the problem, as tax increases often drive taxpayers to other locations, or into tax sheltered activities, while tax cuts often stimulate economic growth and bring in more revenue. Thomas Sowell points out that taxation is not a zero sum game. "The government, which collected less than $50 million in taxes on capital gains in 1924, suddenly collected more than $100 million in capital gains taxes in 1925. At lower tax rates, it no longer made sense to keep so much invested in tax-exempt securities, when more money could be made by investing in the economy."[4]

How bad is it? California: $25.4 billion deficit.[5] Illinois: $13 billion deficit.[6] In all, "2012 is shaping up as states' most difficult budget year on record. Thus far some 44 states and the District of Columbia are projecting budget shortfalls totaling $125 billion for fiscal year 2012."[7] Perhaps that doesn't seem so bad compared to the Fed's $1.5 trillion deficit, but how will the states close this gap without killing their economies?

Remember that "deficit" refers to money already budgeted to spend, but not raised or expected in revenue. It doesn't include unfunded liabilities for things like government union opension plans. "According to the (Moody's) ratings agency, state pensions, which are underfunded by at least $700 billion, face issues that include low returns on investments, an inadequate amount (of) money being saved, the impending retirement of 'baby boomers' born in the late 1940s through the 1960s, and Americans living longer than expected."[8] That's another $700 billion we all owe, but of course, since it is unfunded state liability, some of us owe more than others—unlike with the federal debt and liabilities.

Now the bills for vote buying are due and the revenues have collapsed. The states in the worst shape tend to be those who tried to get golden eggs by killing the goose. "In October, the Tax Foundation rated all 50 states by how their tax climate treated business. California ranked 49th. Only New York rated worse. The foundation also judged that California had the 48th worst individual income tax system and the 49th worst sales tax system. With established businesses fleeing and new entrepreneurs choosing to go elsewhere, unemployment has been trending up in California for four straight years. It is now at 12.4 percent tied with Rust Belt Michigan for the second highest unemployment rate of any state."[9]

As big-government state economies get worse, and they respond by trying to squeeze more eggs from the productive citizens, the tax generators flee and the tax consumers flock to them. "The Census Bureau's 2010 Statistical Abstract says that from 2000 to 2008, 1,378,706 'domestic' migrants left California for other parts of the country. That was balanced by 1,825,697 'international'"migrants (the Census Bureau does not distinguish between legal and illegal) who moved to California from other countries."[9] If you think that improved California's fiscal situation, I can get you a great deal on the Golden Gate Bridge. Extrapolate that in and out migration over ten years, and tell me if you'd like to start a business in California.

As I've noted, raising taxes does not necessarily increase revenue, because—you may want to write this down—people find paying taxes painful. And they are pretty adept at avoiding pain. Take Oregon, for example. "In 2009 the state legislature raised the tax rate to 10.8% on joint-filer income of between $250,000 and $500,000, and to 11% on income above $500,000. Only New York City's rate is higher. ... Instead of $180 million collected last year from the new tax, the state received $130 million ... One reason revenues are so low is that about one-quarter of the rich tax filers seem to have gone missing." [10]

I'm sure it will come as a terrible shock to know that the Federal Government encouraged state and municipal irresponsibility—when it wasn't requiring it through unfunded mandates. For example, the feds offered the states and cities tax-subsidized "Build America Bonds" (BAB) to encourage borrowing. I suppose given the irresponsible borrowing they encouraged in the housing market, this only seemed fair. "States and cities jumped deeply into this new market. California alone has issued some $21 billion in BABs, mostly as a substitute for its general obligation debt to support everything from school construction to sewer projects. New Jersey has used up to $500 million to recapitalize its depleted transportation trust fund. Columbus, Ohio, issued $131 million in BABs to start construction of a downtown convention hotel. And in Dallas, Texas, when no private operator would finance a new convention hotel, the city went ahead with a government-subsidized hotel, courtesy of $388 million in BABs." [11]

The situation is dire enough that increasingly people are floating the idea that somehow we need to let the worst states declare bankruptcy, to escape from their debts and restructure their liabilities. There are problems with this idea, too. A state is a sovereign entity, which makes bankruptcy problematic. And a state bankruptcy would send economic shock waves far beyond the state's borders. So would a state's default on its bonds.

Back when I was in the Massachusetts senate, the Commonwealth under Michael Dukakis faced a massive tax increase to pay for years of vote buying. As a Republican, I hadn't voted to spend the money that now wasn't there. And there were only seven of us in the senate. But the Democrats were having trouble rounding up enough votes among the tax spenders to pay for the spending with new taxes, and Massachusetts was looking at a default. For a time, it looked like I might have to vote for a career-ending tax hike to cover the spending of others, but to spare the citizens the pernicious effect of a default. I was glad the Senate President, the late Kevin Harrington, rounded up the votes in his party.

"A state bankruptcy law would not let creditors thrust a state into bankruptcy that would violate state sovereignty. But it would allow a state government going into bankruptcy to force a 'cram down,' imposing a haircut on bondholders, and to rewrite its union contracts. The threat of bankruptcy would put a powerful weapon in the hands of governors and legislatures: They can tell their unions that they have to accept cuts now or face a much more dire fate in bankruptcy court." [12]

Among the proponents of letting states go bankrupt are former speaker Newt Gingrich and former governor Jeb Bush, who say, "If Californians were given the opportunity to do an end run around the politicians in Sacramento and vote to reform their state government under the U.S. Bankruptcy Code, it would almost certainly trigger a proposition fight. In such a circumstance, the proposition could provide that a yes vote would trigger the cancellation of all state government employee union contracts. Even if the proposition were defeated, the debate surrounding it would make abundantly clear to the people of California and the rest of the country just how much of a stranglehold government employee unions have on state and federal budgets." [13]

Though the alternative may be worse, this is a tricky and scary issue for taxpayers, bankers and investors. "For now, the fear of destabilizing the municipal bond market with the words 'state bankruptcy' has proponents in Congress going about their work on tiptoe. No draft bill is in circulation yet, and no member of Congress has come forward as a sponsor ..." [14]

Not everyone thinks that state bankruptcy is a terrific idea. "Such an option would certainly rattle the bond market—which bankruptcy proponents see as a good thing. Yet this ignores the potential for collateral damage and disruption. While bond spreads might get wider for the most troubled states, the enactment of a state bankruptcy law is likely to raise the cost of borrowing for all municipal issuers." [15]

"Much of the talk about state bankruptcy has centered on the solvency threat posed by unfunded public pension liabilities of as much as $3 trillion, according to an estimate by Joshua Rauh of Northwestern University ... However, while most public pension liabilities are pooled in statewide, off-budget trust funds, they largely reflect the cost of retirement benefits promised to teachers, cops and firefighters—who mainly work for municipalities, not state governments." [15]

I personally think bankruptcy is always a bad idea. I also think smashing on rocks is a bad idea—but the time to think about that is before you step off the cliff.

Unfortunately, the problem doesn't end with the states. A lot of cities are in desperate shape. (I'm sorry if I'm over-using "desperate." It's hard to find superlatives to express the enormity of the situation.) "Overdrawn American cities could face financial collapse in 2011, defaulting on hundreds of billions of dollars of borrowings and derailing the U.S. economic recovery. Nor are European cities safe – Florence, Barcelona, Madrid, Venice: all are in trouble. More than 100 American cities could go bust next year as the debt crisis that has taken down banks and countries threatens next to spark a municipal meltdown, a leading analyst has warned." [16]

How bad is municipal debt? "Since 2000 the total outstanding state and municipal bond debt, adjusted for inflation, has soared from $1.5 trillion to $2.8 trillion. ... The recession didn't slow the spending." [17]

Politicians at the local level have proven as adept at buying votes through debt-financed "games and circuses" as congressmen. It has been going on since the Roman Republic, of course. The New Jersey Sports and Exposition Authority presents a fine example, because " ... the pols couldn't resist soaking the Meadowlands. They siphoned track proceeds into the state budget; repeatedly refinanced the NJSEA's bonds, pushing repayment dates far into the future; and relied on the authority's good credit rating to launch other building schemes ... Today, 35 years after its first bonds, the NJSEA is $830 million in hock. Worse, it can't repay that debt because business has cratered at the racetrack ... As for Giants Stadium, it was demolished this year ... The state, facing its own cavernous budget deficits, has had to assume the authority's interest payments—about $100 million this year on bonds that now stretch out to nearly 2030."[18]

I have a job with a non-profit that has me locked into the Chicago area. I feel like I'm sitting on the edge of a smoldering volcano. As I write, a new Chicago mayor has just been elected, but why anyone would seek election to the post is beyond me, unless it was the chance for enrichment at the public's expense. "Chicago's public pension funds are teetering on the brink of insolvency in large part because city officials and union leaders repeatedly exploited the system, draining away billions of dollars in the last decade to serve short-term political needs ... Time and again, the funds have been used as a bargaining chip or a piggy bank. Politicians trimmed budgets by offering early retirement incentives and greased union contract deals with increases in benefits."[19]

As the situation has worsened, Chicago officials increased their bets, like gamblers at the track trying to get even. "Trustees of Chicago's failing public pension funds have funneled hundreds of millions of dollars into highly speculative investments that not only have failed to realize outsize returns but also saddled them with underperforming, long-term assets that can't be sold off ... The investments, which involved buying equity stakes in businesses ranging from fast-food franchises in Mississippi to a Los Angeles grocery chain, were supposed to plug huge holes in pension fund coffers by yielding gains of up to 20 percent a year."[20]

The fact that I don't actually live in Chicago gives me little hope. Small town America—or at least small city America in many cases—is swirling around the same drain. There are regular reports of unfunded pension liabilities in the "collar communities" around Chicago, due to pension deals the *Chicago Tribune* called suicide pacts. "Often when these retirement deals were cut, the public officials and the union leaders were, in effect, seated on the same side of the negotiating table holding hands. The politicians essentially pledged future tax dollars in return for the cooperation of public sector unions."[21] Pension liabilities have gone up 444% in a decade: "the funding deficit for the 10 largest Chicago-area public pension funds soared from $3.4 billion in 1998 to $18.5 billion in 2008 ... "[22]

State and local governments "employ one in every seven workers, more than manufacturing ..."[23] Once they were allowed to unionize, the power of public employees was put to work to drain the coffers of government at all levels. Given union political power, fixing the problem may be impossible, short of collapse, just as many diseases are only resolved with the death of the patient.

Looking again at Illinois, "Despite the dire financial condition of his state, and the fact that it was (and still is) a sovereign deadbeat that fails to pay its bills, Illinois Democratic Gov. Pat Quinn found room to cut a sweetheart deal with its public employee unions in September. They were guaranteed two years of cost-of-living increases and no layoffs. Quinn, in turn, got the union's endorsement and won his 2010 election by less than 1 percentage point." [24]

Can the gaps be closed by taxes? Illinois raised its state income taxes by 67% and its corporate tax rate by 46% to 7%, fourth highest in the nation, a move that will likely drive jobs and revenues out of the state. But the, "new revenues will produce $6.5 billion. That amount has to cover a $15 billion budget deficit. Failing a miracle of loaves and fishes, it won't work." [25]

My own property taxes increased 33% last year, though the assessment on our condo came down from $210,000 to $167,500, close to the purchase price of $160,000. Next year, my tax bill says I can expect another 55% hike. And the Cook County sales tax has just come down to 9.75% from 10.25%, highest in the country. There aren't a lot of eggs left in the dying taxpayer goose here, as elsewhere.

What about other cities?

"Detroit Public Schools would close nearly half of its schools in the next two years, and increase high school class sizes to 62 by the following year, under a deficit-reduction plan filed with the state ... to slash a $327 million deficit in the district to zero over the next several years." [26] That's just the school system. The city's long term debt has hit $5.7 billion. [27]

"As San Francisco struggles under ballooning pension and health care costs, the city's retirees will receive unexpected cost-of-living bonuses totaling $170 million. The city's anticipated budget deficit for the coming year is $360 million ... The special $170 million bonus is in excess of regular cost-of-living adjustments, or COLAs ... the $13.1 billion San Francisco Employees' Retirement System now had an unfunded liability of $1.6 billion — triple its shortfall a year earlier." [28]

"New York City's projected budget deficit for fiscal 2012 may widen by $2 billion, to $4.5 billion ..." [29]

Prosperous, pro-business Texas is, of course, a bright spot. In Dallas, the deficit estimate is much lower. "City Manager Mary Suhm calculates that ... the city will be $41 million in the hole as it seeks to balance revenues and expenditures in 2011-12. In the worst case, that number jumps to a deficit of $96 million." [30] Compared to many other cities, that's bake-sale size. But it's still a problem.

A lot of small burgs are in bad shape, but don't get as much national attention—until things go really wrong. Camden, NJ, is a small city across the river from Philadelphia, where in 1964 I enlisted in the Marines. It's next to Collingswood, where I went to high school, and my grandfather and great-grandmother are buried there. It's been a disaster for years, but now has hit the national news by laying off police. "One of America's most dangerous cities, Camden seeks to close a $26.5 million budget hole by laying off one-quarter of its city government workers—including half of its police force. In an austerity plan that went into effect last month, the city laid off 180 uniformed officers and 20 police dispatchers from its 375-strong force." [31]

That's what a collapse will look like. No police to deal with the rising tide of thugs. " ... the reduction of sworn officers within our Police and Fire Departments will result in a severe public safety crisis affecting residents, workers and visitors." [31] When I lived in South Jersey ten years ago, a goodly number of Camden's visitors were there to buy drugs in the city's open-air drug markets. It will only get worse.

Then there are the quasi-government agencies, which have quietly been building up debt for years. Back in 2007, when the economy was much better, the Chicago Transit Authority was facing "a $1.5 billion hole in its stash of assets ... At the height of a four-year bull market, it didn't have enough cash on hand to pay its retirees through 2013, meaning it was underfunded to the tune of 62 percent." [32] To fix that, it decided to borrow money. " ... the CTA ignored the warning and issued $1.9 billion in bonds. Before the year ended, the pension fund was paying out more to bondholders than it was earning on its new influx of money." [32]

How many more of these fiscal time bombs are ticking away around the country?

But no matter how bad things get, the public employee monster must be fed, or they will turn on their political masters. "Montgomery County Chief Administrative Officer Timothy Firestine earns more than $266,000 annually, and Fairfax County Executive Anthony Griffin nets $240,000even with pay freezes. D.C. City Administrator Neil Albert, who also fills an appointed position, makes $225,000. ... Outgoing Montgomery County Schools Superintendent Jerry Weast, for example, earned nearly $500,000 this year ..." [33] They are just following the shining example from the federal level of how to cope with an economic downturn and soaring deficits. The rest of the country may have experienced a recession, but government employees have not. "The number of federal workers earning $150,000 or more a year has soared tenfold in the past five years and doubled since President Obama took office ..." [34]

And the government employees are united and powerful. Tax dollars go into their pockets, and they are determined to keep them flowing. "The message was consistent: Freezing federal salaries, cutting benefits and shrinking the workforce will not balance the federal budget. Such moves will hurt low-paid civil servants in every member's district. Service will worsen." [35]

The information presented in these first two chapters is not intended to be a comprehensive list of the fiscal problems facing governments at all levels. I don't have the space here, the time or, frankly, the heart to try to compile a definitive list. And I doubt it's possible, with news of worsening situations hitting my inbox daily.

Yes, I'm cherry picking many worst-case articles. I urge you to spend some time in Internet research looking at various governments' fiscal challenges. I'm sure you will find some bright spots. But I'm equally sure they will be negated by one story after another of looming fiscal disaster.

Could we cope with this growing fiscal mess? Of course, though it would take extensive self sacrifice on the part of everyone, something Americans no longer seem interested in or capable of. I mean everyone. It is probably impossible in a culture where for years the political game has been a "pass the pain" version of musical chairs to see who else your group can stick with the costs to keep your benefits flowing. In most cases, it has been future taxpayers—but the future is here.

Unfortunately, the fiscal problem, immense as it is, isn't our only problem. There are at least three other major dangers that feed that problem, and make it exponentially more challenging to deal with. as you read Chapters three, Four and Five, remember we must try to cope with those problems with a government that is critically short of money and an economy that is staggering.

The first of these is immigration policy.

Chapter Three: Destroying America through Immigration

Having an intelligent conversation about immigration policy has become almost impossible. Mention it, and immigrant support groups, leftist politicians and their mainstream media water-carriers immediately brand you a racist, even though you oppose illegal immigration of folks of your own race and welcome legal immigration of folks of other races. Once you are stuck with that tar baby—if quoting Joel Chandler Harris's *Uncle Remus* doesn't confirm the accusation—you spend all your energy trying to disentangle yourself . And like Br'er Rabbit, everything you do is used to bind you tighter to their narrative about you. Try saying, "Some of my best friends are...." Better you should have no friends, because like denying you are an alcoholic, every denial of racism is cited as proof, and the discussion becomes about your flaws, not about the issue. It is a very effective and destructive tactic to focus the debate on you and thus avoid the issue.

In 2009, I wrote a blog piece entitled "I'm Tired" which went viral on the Internet. In it I wrote, "I'm tired of illegal aliens being called 'undocumented workers,' especially the ones who aren't working, but are living on welfare or crime. What's next? Calling drug dealers, 'Undocumented Pharmacists'? And, no, I'm not against Hispanics. Most of them are Catholic and it's been a few hundred years since Catholics wanted to kill me for my religion. I'm willing to fast track for citizenship any Hispanic person who can speak English, doesn't have a criminal record and who is self-supporting without a family on welfare, or who serves honorably for three years in our military. Those are the citizens we need."

For that statement, which would get me labeled as being a "RINO" (republican in Name only) who supports "amnesty" on some right-wing sites, I was branded a racist numerous times in blog comments. And a few overly sensitive Catholics misunderstood my perhaps-clumsy reference to the fact that Protestants and Catholics had long been at peace to take offence as well, demonstrating how difficult rationality is in this area. Or that being offended and playing "gotcha" is a game far too many enjoy.

At the risk of confirming the view that I'm a racist, let me say that America has millions of excellent citizens of Hispanic ancestry, whose work ethic and family orientation have enriched our culture. I am well aware that the casualty lists from Iraq and Afghanistan have many Hispanic names among the dead. In many cases, it is Juan and Maria who are serving in place of Jason and Tiffany from our upscale neighborhoods and Ivy League colleges, where military service to the Republic is denigrated among the elites whose grandfathers led our forces in WWII. The Census Bureau reports 1.1 million American veterans of Hispanic heritage.[1]

We should welcome *more* of the right kind of Hispanic immigration, given that they are the main group holding America's birthrate at about the replacement rate of 2.1 live births per woman, while the rest of the civilized world is in a demographic decline toward cultural oblivion.

Nevertheless, at the risk of being shunned by all right-thinking people, and cutting myself off from invitations to white wine and brie parties in Hyde Park, I think illegal immigration by large numbers of Hispanics *and others* is a huge problem for the country, and feeds into both cultural collapse and the fiscal collapse discussed in Chapters One and Two. And if the culture collapses, America then is no longer the America immigrants seek—and will no longer be the prosperous and free place we all desire.

Unfortunately, *illegal* immigration by Mexicans and others is only a part of our immigration problem. But let's discuss that part of the problem first, before the mob with the tar and feathers gets here.

If you think we need open borders, with no enforcement of "racist" immigration restrictions at all, you should be required to open your home to as many "undocumented workers" as wish to live there. No restrictions on numbers may be placed and the undocumented immigrants must be allowed to invite as many family members and friends to join them as wish to come. And those to invite others.

The new residents in your home will, of course, be expected to find jobs if they can, and to pay for as much of their own expenses as possible. But for those who cannot or will not find employment, or for those who can find only low-paid employment (those famous "jobs Americans won't do"), you as the home owner and host will have to pay the difference so they and their children have adequate food, clothing, utilities, health care, education, transportation and other necessities of life to keep them from abject poverty.

This will be expensive, as the definitions of "necessity" and "poverty" have changed. By 2003, "91 percent of those in the lowest 10 percent of households — all officially poor — own color TVs, 74 percent own microwave ovens, 55 percent own VCRs, 47 percent own clothes dryers, 42 percent own stereos, 23 percent own dishwashers, 21 percent own computers and 19 percent own garbage disposals. When I grew up in the 1950s, only the wealthy owned color TVs, clothes dryers, stereos, dishwashers and disposals."[2] Don't expect to skimp on your undocumented guests, even as news of your generosity spreads and ever more join them in your home.

And if at any point you say, "No, enough!" you will be immediately labeled a racist and barred from polite society as surely as an Arizona politician.

This is ridiculous, you say? Your family's culture, lifestyle, standard of living and finances would all rapidly collapse, even as family members who were able to would flee the bedlam your liberal principles have created, in order to seek other domiciles. Exactly.

For that is exactly what unrestricted immigration and open borders will do to the nation's culture, lifestyle, standard of living and finances. Of course, it will take longer, because the country is immensely larger than your household.

Immensely larger, but not infinitely larger. At some point, the place to which the immigrants are coming will no longer be culturally, politically or financially the America to which they now want to immigrate. Neither they, nor the inhabitants here to greet them will be especially happy with the changes.

Could America absorb as citizens the estimated 11.2 million "unauthorized migrants" living in the United States?[3] Yes, though not painlessly. But suppose we fulfilled the dreams of these 11 million souls, plus the dreams of Democratic Party strategists who would count on getting a large proportion of their votes as entitlement-dependent voters, and made them all citizens in a blanket amnesty, as some suggest? Tomorrow, the first of the next ten million "unauthorized migrants" would arrive. About 9% of the current undocumented migrants arrived from 2008 to 2010. That flood would increase as word of the amnesty spread—why should they not expect the same largess in five or ten years?

Illegal immigrants increase the population through a high birth rate as well. "Births to unauthorized immigrant parents accounted for 8% of newborns from March 2009 to March 2010," but, "unauthorized immigrants made up 3.7% of the nation's population."[3]

Given that without Hispanic immigrants, America would be in the same demographic death-spiral as Europe and Japan, thanks to the availability of birth control and abortion as well as the current fashion for small families to preserve affluent life-styles, we certainly need Hispanic and other immigrants. By 2050, it is projected that there will be 132 million Hispanics in the United States.[1] If we have 132 million *Americans* of Hispanic ancestry, it will be wonderful. If we have 132 millions Mexicans and others who are culturally and emotionally embedded in the country they left behind, it will be a disaster. It is unlikely, of course, to be 100% either way—but will the proportion be high enough for America to remain America? Or will the dream of a *reconquista* of California and the Southwest—attributed to and denied by La Raza and other Hispanic groups—become a reality?

We need the right kind of immigrants. And, no, I'm not talking about their racial, ethnic or religious heritage, though I fully expect this statement to be taken out of context to prove my venality—that is what the Left does. But we do need immigrants, regardless of race or ethnicity, who want to become *Americans*, not those who want to re-establish here the failed cultures and corrupt political systems they fled. Nor do we need to allow in criminal elements from the drug cartels who see us as prey. We are quite capable of growing our own gangs, thank you.

Americans have an affluent lifestyle, based on political freedom, limited government, property rights and a tolerant culture. Immigrants who have the desire and ability to join that culture will enrich us all. Those who want to bring the corruption, poverty, oppression and intolerance of the third world here, or who want to feed on our affluence without becoming part of our culture, will, if allowed, destroy everything good that we have and that most immigrants seek. We aid them to our peril. We have enough challenges with the alternative government-and-crime-dependent culture that has grown up in our cities, which threatens us from within, without importing the seeds of our destruction. If you don't believe me, look at Mexico, a country rich in natural resources and agricultural potential. Which way do the immigrants flow? Why have they not built a society close to ours? Hint: it's not about race.

Look at the changes in language and culture in the past thirty years, due to immigration. If you are over 40, for much of your life there was no, "Press Two for Spanish."

Press Two for Racism

If you treat one group of people better and another group of people worse purely because of their race or ethnic background, isn't that racism? If so, then having Spanish on everything from corporation voice-mail hells to government programs is clearly racist. After all, there are a lot of citizens, permanent residents and, yes, illegal immigrants whose native language is something other than English or Spanish. That immigrants from Mexico and other Hispanic countries, legal or illegal, get to have everything presented in their native language while immigrants from Poland or Vietnam or Latvia or China do not, *clearly* discriminates in a racist way against those immigrants who come from a non-Hispanic culture.

Is it because there are more Hispanic immigrants than those from other language groups? So you can discriminate if a group is a minority, and it's okay? Since English-speaking whites (currently) outnumber other groups, by the "Press two for Spanish" logic, it's okay to discriminate against those other groups. Given our litigation-happy culture, it won't be long before a smarmy lawyer figures that out and decides to cast aside political correctness in favor of a payoff. Then we will see the courts tied in knots trying to promote "fairness"— that liberal chimera—for everyone.

The worst part is that the practice discriminates against Hispanics as well. I have read that Hispanics who speak only Spanish earn significantly lower incomes than those who speak English, though because of the bilingual demand, those who speak both do best of all. But by making it easier for Hispanic immigrants to get by without learning English, we condemn them to poverty and welfare dependence. That, of course may be the point for political groups that depend on the government-dependent for their power base.

And by promoting a bilingual society, you promote conflict within that society. Yes, there are peaceful societies, like Switzerland, where there are more than one dominant language. But there are many examples, like Quebec and Belgium, where it leads to political rancor, and sometimes violence, perhaps even disunion. A common language is a unifying force, while bilingualism is a Balkanizing force. In the face of the challenges before us, we need all the unifying we can get.

America is a great country and a wonderful place to live, not because of the dominant race, but because of the dominant culture, which promotes hard work, self-sufficiency, individualism, private property and integrity. (Don't laugh. If we have corruption here, at least we abhor and fight it. In all too many cultures, it is accepted and expected. And the corruptocracies are always backward in economics and human rights.) We also have long exposure to the benefits of free markets and property rights, the foundations of economic advancement. And, yes, these are the widely-derided values of the so-called Protestant Ethic— or of the hated Bourgeoisie.

Of course, both politicians and activists in Hispanic groups have a strong self-interest in keeping Hispanic immigrants from integrating into American culture. Only if Hispanics view themselves as a separate and victimized minority can these "leaders" be assured of their support. The same dynamic is at work among too many black "leaders" and white politicians dependent on black votes, who are perfectly content to have a large, suffering subculture of black folks living in misery and dependence, in order to maintain their own positions.

There is also support for illegal immigration among those who benefit from cheaper labor, whether business people or elites seeking cheap domestic help and child care, though they may not be as supportive of Hispanics living next to them in their gated communities. There is support from political groups who want to garner votes and financial support from citizens who belong to the same migrant groups and, perhaps, from newly-minted voters. The bitter joke is that these are not "Illegal Immigrants," but "Undocumented Democrats." This ignores the fact that many Republican politicians have pandered to Hispanic groups on immigration as well. It puts many public officials in the interesting position of urging non-enforcement of laws they cannot change, and would not dare vote to change if they could.

And illegal immigration keeps wages low in some occupations, thus creating the self-fulfilling prophesy of "jobs Americans won't do."

This is hardly a new problem. Back in 1993, a leading U.S. Senator said, "Our federal wallet is stretched to the limit by illegal aliens getting welfare, food stamps, medical care and other benefits, often without paying taxes. Safeguards like welfare and free medical care are in place to boost Americans in need of short-term assistance. These programs were not meant to entice freeloaders and scam artists from around the world." [4] His name was Harry Reid, but that was before Hispanic groups became such an important constituency to his party.

What are the fiscal costs of illegal immigration to the nation? It's very hard to quantify, and is offset somewhat by the economic activity they generate. But there is no question that the flood of immigrants contributes to poverty. "First-generation Hispanic immigrants and their families now comprise 9 percent of the U.S. population but 17 percent of all poor persons in the U.S.; and children in Hispanic immigrant families now comprise 11.7 percent of all children in the U.S. but 22 percent of all poor children in the U.S. Massive low-skill immigration works to counteract government anti-poverty efforts. While government works to reduce the number of poor persons, low-skill immigration pushes the poverty numbers up. In addition, low-skill immigration siphons off government anti-poverty funding and makes government efforts to shrink poverty less effective. Low-skill immigrants pay little in taxes and receive high levels of government benefits and services." [5]

How is illegal immigration impacting education? As I noted in Chapter

Two, the states and cities are broke, which means that massive cuts in education funding will be forced on us. Meanwhile, by 2004 "The total K-12 school expenditure for illegal immigrants costs the states nearly $12 billion annually, and when the children born here to illegal aliens are added, the costs more than double to $28.6 billion."[6] You can see how these disasters reinforce each other.

It's hard to get a handle on the social, emotional and financial costs of crimes by illegal immigrants. It appears not to be well tracked, perhaps because the authorities and the mainstream media fear having the "racism" charge hung around their necks. But just as it's true that the majority of legal and illegal immigrants are decent people trying to make a better life for themselves, it's also true that crime and its costs have been rising due to the influx of criminals mixed into the immigrant population. Given that Mexico is on the verge of being a failed state due to the drug cartels, it is only going to get worse.

One area where there are data is in the prison population. "In 1980, our Federal and state facilities held fewer than 9,000 criminal aliens. But at the end of 2003, approximately 267,000 non-citizens were incarcerated in U.S. correctional facilities, as follows: 46,000 in Federal prisons, 74,000 in state prisons, 147,000 in local jails. Approximately 27 percent of all prisoners in Federal custody are criminal aliens. The majority (63 percent) are citizens of Mexico."[7]

These are the ones caught, convicted and incarcerated at taxpayer expense. The cost of their crimes and of the crimes of those not apprehended is immense, and feeds the fiscal disaster as well as our economic problems. Note that these statistics are from 2005. Since then the drug wars in Mexico have pushed more immigrants to the States and inserted more immigrant criminals here as the cartels sought to secure their U.S. markets—or the losers sought safety and new territory for crime.

Given the escalating war in Mexico with tens of thousands of dead, the fear of crime will drive illegal immigration as much as poverty, and criminal immigration will only increase. In my view, anyone in the United States who uses illegal drugs is an accessory to murder. And to the coming collapse of our nation, especially as, "a new Pentagon study concludes that Mexico is at risk of becoming a failed state. Defense planners liken the situation to that of Pakistan, where wholesale collapse of civil government is possible."[8] There are differences, of course. Pakistan is not on our border—but it does have more nuclear weapons than Great Britain. Thankfully, the cartels are not that well armed. Yet.

How about welfare? The following citation includes all immigrants: "As a result of their high rate of poverty, immigrant households are more likely to participate in practically every one of the major means-tested programs. In 2007, immigrant use of welfare programs (32.7 percent) was 69 percent higher than non-immigrants' use (19.4 percent). Each year, state governments spend an estimated $11 billion to $22 billion to provide welfare to immigrants."[9]

What are the costs to the Federal Government? "Households headed by illegal aliens imposed more than $26.3 billion in costs on the federal government in 2002 and paid only $16 billion in taxes, creating a net fiscal deficit of almost $10.4 billion, or $2,700 per illegal household. Among the largest costs are Medicaid ($2.5 billion); treatment for the uninsured ($2.2 billion); food assistance programs such as food stamps, WIC, and free school lunches ($1.9 billion); the federal prison and court systems ($1.6 billion); and federal aid to schools ($1.4 billion)."[10] You will note the federal costs include prisons, already counted above. No need to double count these billions.

Would amnesty help? "If illegal aliens were given amnesty and began to pay taxes and use services like households headed by legal immigrants with the same education levels, the estimated annual net fiscal deficit would increase from $2,700 per household to nearly $7,700, for a total net cost of $29 billion." [10] These numbers are from the Center for Immigration Studies. Their fact-based, non-inflammatory language and policy conclusions are especially worth reading in their entirety. The URL for their website is in the chapter references.

How much faith should you have in all these numbers? The truth is, I don't know. You can certainly find pro-immigration groups who will tear them down, and almost everyone putting together numbers—especially estimates—has a political agenda. Perhaps it is only half or two-thirds as bad as these numbers suggest. Is that comforting?

But you can apply reason. Return to my analogy of the generous liberal who, instead of just opening our country to unlimited undocumented migrants, opens his home, come one, come all. How likely do you think it would be that the folks who would take him up on his offer would be a net plus, financially, culturally or socially? What would his chances be of admitting at least one criminal who would accelerate the fiscal bleeding process, or of one "undocumented pharmaceutical distributor" who would infect his family?

In the face of this invasion, we are in retreat, now erecting anti-illegal-immigrant and drug smuggling barriers 70 miles inside our borders.[11] The costs are unsustainable. Welfare costs for the parents of "anchor babies" are now estimated to be $600 million per year.[12] Not in the country—in just Los Angeles, one city. Imagine again it's your home, your bank account is empty, creditors are calling—and you have ceded the porch and part of the living room to your undocumented guests.

It is beyond wishful thinking to assume that our open border can contain the violence in Mexico. "Last year in Ciudad Juárez, the Mexican city across from El Paso, some 3,111 civilians were murdered while in all of Afghanistan 2,421 civilians were killed. On a per capita basis, a civilian was 30 times more likely to be murdered last year in Juárez, a city of 1.3 million people, than in Afghanistan, with its 29.1 million people." [13] El Paso is not far away from you— modern transportation means a criminal there today can be on your doorstep tomorrow.

Unfortunately, even legal immigration is a huge problem, thanks to changes in our immigration laws. We no longer select those who want to become Americans, who want to assimilate, who can contribute economically, rather than take from the economy. "... the immigration reform act of 1965 ...

abolished with a single stroke the principle of maintaining America's previous ethnic balance, and opened wide the doors to newcomers from all around the world, with entry based not on ethnicity or even one's perceived economic value to the U.S., but rather on the principle of 'family reunification.' Unthinkingly, we set up a system that encouraged large, extended families of largely uneducated migrants to flood onto our shores, at precisely the time our industrial growth had begun to stagnate, our farms had become mostly mechanized, and our civic culture lost the self-confidence required to assimilate anyone."[14]

Meantime, our immigration policies actually keep out the highly skilled immigrants who would help revitalize our economy thus making America stronger in the face of these challenges. "Our economy grows by the efforts of the nation's entrepreneurs and workers — but only if they have enough freedom. Immigration restrictions on highly skilled workers restrict that freedom in the most fundamental sense. Punishing highly educated and skilled workers with regulations and a low (immigration limit) also hurts Americans. First, foreign highly skilled workers do not 'take' American jobs. The economy doesn't have a set number of jobs. Rather, jobs are created and destroyed based on production possibilities and economic innovation. Foreign workers are also consumers and investors, increasing employment opportunities for Americans."[15]

We are hardly alone in having lost the will to control our borders. "In 2009 some 3,600 migrants managed to slip across the frontier not far from this market town; in 2010 that number shot up to 36,000, helping explain why Greece has become the favoured port of entry for 90% of illegals pouring into the EU."[16]

"Modern immigration regimes are causing similar problems in all Western countries, whether Holland, Denmark, France, Sweden or Canada—or Britain. As for the UK, as the Muslim population continues to grow, its culture will become more Islamized, no matter what is done within the confines of British democracy."[17]

Of course. Europe's problem is not primarily illegal Hispanic Catholics, but illegal Muslims from the Middle East and North Africa who are even less likely to want to assimilate, and more likely to be committed to the destruction of the host culture. A member of a Mexican drug cartel who comes to the United States is a blood sucking parasite who wants to feed upon the host, not kill it. An Islamic supremacist who migrates to Germany, France, Britain, Holland or Sweden wants to destroy the freedoms, culture and religion there and replace it with the *Dar al-Islam* as part of the promised Caliphate.

Let us turn to the Jihad.

Chapter Four: The Twin Jihads—Working in Tandem to Wreck the Republic

(Note that most Islamic terms come from the Arabic, which may be rendered in English in several ways. For example, Islamic Law often appears as *Sharia*, *Shariah*, *Shari'a*, etc. I've used spellings that seemed reasonable to me.)

If illegal immigration is a difficult subject to broach, having a serious, rational discussion about the subject of Islamist Terror and the Twin Jihads is even more challenging. Any attempt to do so not only opens you up to the usual *ad hominem* attack of racism, with "Islamophobia" thrown in for good measure, but to the threat of violence and death. (Infidel! You have insulted Islam by saying some Muslims are violent. *Insha'Allah*, we will kill you to avenge the insult!) These are excellent tactics for diverting attention from the problem by forcing those who want to deal realistically with the threat to defend themselves, verbally, legally and sometimes physically.

Is being concerned about terror and jihad racist? If it is, Islam is the only race you can join. Anyone can become a Muslim by sincerely making the "Declaration of Faith" (the *Shahada*) that is one of the *Five Pillars of Islam*. Simply say, "There is no other god but Allah and Muhammad is the last messenger of God." Or as it's often rendered, "...and Mohammad is his Prophet." Instantly, you are a now a Muslim (and anyone who criticizes you is racist—or at least "Islamophobic").

"Islamophobia" was invented because it was hard to stick a charge of "racism" on critics when anyone could make a simple statement and become a member of your "race." The term pre-dated the mass murders of September 11, 2001, but it came into common usage as a pejorative to silence critics of Islamic terrorists after that date.[1] Though there had been a long string of jihadist murders and attacks on America[2] and the West prior to that attack, the 9/11 horror was so bad that to defend its perpetrators a special epithet was needed. Thus "Islamophobia" entered the popular culture. The chances are you never heard that term while the Twin Towers stood.

And when you hear it now, you may be reasonably sure it is being used to *silence* a critic of Islamic extremism, which thus avoids real discussion of the issue, just as charges of "racism" are used to turn discussion away from the issue of illegal immigration or from the issues the Tea Party protesters are concerned about. It is an attempt to intimidate people concerned about the future into not exercising their First Amendment rights.

What is "Islamophobia?" Wikipedia says, " ... the British Runnymede Trust defined Islamophobia as the 'dread or hatred of Islam and therefore, to the fear and dislike of all Muslims,'" and "the practice of ... excluding them from ... economic, social, and public life ..." Also, " ... the perception that Islam has no values in common with other cultures, is inferior to the West and is a violent political ideology rather than a religion."[1]

So to be "Islamophobic," you must fear and dread "all Muslims"? That lets almost everyone off the hook. As to the perceptions about Islam, we must note there is no one "Islam" any more than Christianity or Judaism is a monolith. One might have negative perceptions of the beliefs of Copts or Catholics or of reform Jews, without being "Christophobic" or "Jewophobic." Those terms, of course, are not much in use. Especially in Islamic countries, it is perfectly acceptable to criticize, condemn, attack with vicious lies and discriminate against Christian or Jews. Doing so doesn't earn the attackers any opprobrium from the UN, the courts, various "human rights" tribunals, the Left or their sycophants in the mainstream media.

The above definition is so broad as to allow me and most readers to absolve ourselves of the charge, regardless of how those who would minimize the threats of the Twin Jihads will throw it at us to stifle discussion. Note that they twist any criticism of some of the values of some versions of Islam into, "Islam has no values in common with other cultures." Of course, all movements have *some* values in common and some that are exclusive to them, and often repellant to others. National Socialism believed in having teens get outside and exercise in the Nazi Youth movements. Finding that common value with our culture does not make the Third Reich one of the great forces for peace and good in the world, however much certain groups—dare I say which ones?—would like to finish the work the Nazis started.

I have neither the space nor the expertise to get into an extended discussion of what Islam is or is not, but I will touch on the more radical versions which are both political and religious systems, and have many values—if not all—that are the antithesis of freedom and western civilization. In "Chapter Eight: What You Can Do to Prevent a Collapse" I offer a minimal reading list for educated voters that includes books praising and criticizing Islam. The appendix on resources offers links to websites that go into detail about Islam. Given that we will be engaged with both moderate and extremist Muslims for the foreseeable future, it is worth the time to educate yourself on the views of both sides.

But for clarity, here's how I see Islam and Muslims.

Islam is many discrete "religions" falling under a general heading, much as Christianity and Judaism have many parts, some benign, some distinctly unattractive. Just as the Papacy, the Amish and the Westboro Baptist Church share some beliefs, so they have many fundamental, probably irreconcilable differences. One of the tenets of Islam held by many Islamic scholars of all stripes is that the *Qur'an* is the unchangeable commands of God or Allah, given to his final messenger, Mohammad, and as such is not subject to re-interpretation or updating in any way. "Ninety per cent of the *Shari'a* consists of the incontestable matters and essentials of religion, each of which is a diamond pillar. Only ten per cent are matters open to interpretation, controversial, and secondary ..."[3]

In point of fact, there are many interpretations of Islam: Sunni and Shi'a, Sufi and Wahabi, Salafist and Druze, among others. That each considers Muslims who believe in other interpretations to be apostates from the "True Islam" has led to endless trouble and bloodshed, ever since the Shi'a—or was it the Sunni—went astray over Mohammad's successor. In point of fact, most of the victims of Islamic terror and violence have been fellow Muslims who had strayed from the True Path—as the killer defined it. Muslims have slaughtered fellow Muslims in intramural violence in far greater numbers than anything envisioned by the most "Islamophobic" *kuffer* (infidel). On any given day, the victims of Allah-murders are most likely to be Muslims.

Neither I nor most of the readers of this small volume "dread and hate" all forms of Islam, nor "fear and dislike" all Muslims. Both apologists and critics of Islam err if they do not differentiate between the various forms of Islam, as hateful as that concept will be to most Islamic scholars who recognize only one Islam—the one that happens to be theirs.

Let me define what and who I do dread, hate, fear and dislike. I dread and hate all interpretations of Islam that say Islam must be imposed on the world, by force if necessary, and that Muslims must rule non-Muslims. I fear and hate those who say the anti-freedom values enshrined in *Shari'a* law must replace the values of liberty and western civilization enshrined in our Constitution and traditions. I fear and dislike those Muslims who seek to impose those anti-freedom values on the rest of us, by whatever means, be it terror, the courts, laws or temporary recourse to democracy when it suits their anti-democratic purpose. Prime Minister Erdogan of "moderate," EU-membership-candidate Turkey has been quoted as saying, "Democracy is like a train. We shall get out when we arrive at the station we want." [4] It may not be an accurate quote, but clearly there are many who would use democratic means to eliminate democracy in favor of an Islamist theocracy. They must be fought, not least on behalf of the millions of Muslims who want to live in peace and freedom, free of the worst excesses of *Shari'a*.

We are not at war with Islam as a whole. But we are certainly at war with those forms of Islam that teach and work toward Islamic supremacy. We are at war with those versions of Islam that wish to destroy Western freedom and replace it with those anti-freedom aspects of the *Qur'an*, the *Hadith* (*Sunna*) and *Shari'a*. We are at war because they are at war with us—and it takes only one side to make a war, but two to make a peace. ("Peace Activists" busy feeling warm and fuzzy about themselves, might want to write that down.) It's telling that much of Islamic thought divides the world into two parts, the *Dar al-Islam* (the World of Islam or "Submission," those countries that have submitted to Islamic rule) and the *Dar al-Harb* (the World of War, those countries under infidel rule). That many Muslims call the non-Islamic world the "World of *War*" reinforces the view of critics that Islam preaches conquest of non-Muslims.

All Muslims are not our enemies. The majority of Muslims are not our enemies. But those Muslims who seek to impose laws and requirements on our society that are antithetical to freedom are our enemies. It doesn't matter if their methods are violent terror or non-violent agitation, propaganda, law suits and disinformation in the mainstream media, they have made themselves our enemies. I believe that the majority of the world's 1.3 billion Muslims want only to live in peace and to make better lives for their families. I believe that is true of the vast majority of American Muslims.

I also believe that the vast majority of Germans and Japanese in 1939 wanted to live in peace and make better lives for their families. Unfortunately, they were mostly irrelevant, because the extremists had the guns and the power. Those who weren't irrelevant and spoke out died violently at the hands of the extremists. And while freedom has had support from moderate, peaceful Muslims, they are too often irrelevant, cowed or controlled by those with the guns, just as the Germans and Japanese were in 1939.

These extreme Muslims have been called Islamic Supremacists or Islamists. I prefer to call them Jihadists—those waging Jihad to subjugate the world to their vision of Islam. It will never happen, of course, can't happen, because there are many Jihadist visions—and they will murder each other as they get more power. But the establishment of Islamic terror-theocracies like Iran is possible, not only in today's Muslim majority countries, but in the coming Muslim majority in Europe. And they dream of an Islamic Republic of America. "British radical Muslim activist Anjem Choudary made clear what he and his Islamist brothers have planned for the West. 'We do believe, as Muslims, the East and the West will one day be governed by the *Shariah*,' he said. 'Indeed, we believe that one day, the flag of Islam will fly over the White House." [5]

This may not be the view of a majority of Muslims, but neither is it the view of only a "tiny minority of extremists who have hijacked a great religion," as the apologist cliché has it. The fact is, we don't know what percent of Muslims are Jihadists who wish to impose *Shari'a* law—or some aspects of *Shari'a*—on the rest of us, by whatever means. I may not be Islamophobic, but I'm certainly Jihadophobic. And Naziophobic, Communistophobic and Chicago-street-gang-ophobic, while we're at it.

Jihadism varies from those who are eager to die for Allah via suicide bomb, taking as many *kuffer* (infidels) and apostate Muslims with them as possible, to those who are peaceful fellow citizens who happen to quietly believe it would be great if Islam was forced on everybody, and are willing to help the work toward that goal. Just as Islam is not monolithic, neither is Jihadism. Unfortunately, a majority of Muslims in many Islamic countries support many of the oppressive principles of *Shari'a* law that are incompatible with freedom.

The Jihadists are not a unified enemy controlled by a central command, a fact that makes them far more difficult to defeat than, for example, Nazi Germany. Rather, they are hundreds of groups and tens (or hundreds) of thousands of individuals who believe that Islam is destined to rule all of humanity under *Shari'a* law and it is their duty to Allah to advance that goal by all the means at hand.

True, there are Christians, Jews and doubtless folks of other faiths who would like to see tenets of their religions enshrined into law. But they aren't working in tandem with a violent wing of their faith, and using that to obtain concessions. If your morning paper carries a report of an attack on a place of worship or a suicide bombing, do you immediately suspect that it was done by Buddhists or Presbyterians or Jews in the name of their God? No, you assume it was Jihadists—and 99.9% of the time, you are right.

And that is what I call the Twin Jihad. One wing is composed of the violent groups, who use murder to cow people into making concessions that advance their political goals. These are the terrorist organizations like al Qaeda, Hamas, Hizbollah, al-Shabaab, the Taliban, MILF, Jamaat-e-Islami and many others. It includes their state sponsors, such as Iran, and state agencies such as a good part of the ISI in Pakistan. It also includes those Muslims who "go Jihad" and carry out freelance attacks on non-believers or fellow Muslims they see as apostates, an increasing threat in America.

The other wing uses the violent wing as a lever to push for what has been called "The Stealth Jihad."

That includes those who raise funds for the terrorists, and seek to divert attention from them, to make their paths easier or to cover their activities. Groups such as the Council on Islamic-American Relations (CAIR) in the United States are alleged to have ties to violent groups recognized as terrorist, like Hamas.[7] (See the link to "Extremism and the Council on American-Islamic Relations (CAIR)" in the chapter references. See also *Stealth Jihad*[8])

Step by step, the stealth Jihadists demand changes in American and western society to advance their view of Islam. Some of these have been extreme and laughable, like replacing the Statute of Liberty with a minaret, and covering it with a burka until that can be done, so as not to offend Muslims.[9] But such ridiculous demands have a sinister purpose, making the small steps toward *Shari'a* Law seem reasonable. It has seemed easier to make small concessions than to fight everything, easier to restrict freedom of speech to avoid offending some Muslims.

Which is why we have Muslim foot baths installed at the Kansas City Airport[10] and at some universities,[11] Muslim calls to prayer broadcast daily in Michigan,[12] and Muslim cab drivers who have refused to transport passengers carrying alcohol or with guide dogs, considered "unclean" in Islam,[13] in violation of Americans' civil rights. It is why some American students "learn the 'five pillars' of Islam, study Ramadan and listen to guest speakers including an American Muslim who arrived dressed in her religious costume to talk to the kids about her Quran."[14] This has been upheld by courts that would strike down such teachings about Christianity and the Bible, which properly belong in church.

These are, indeed, small steps, none of which threaten the foundations of the Republic. But they are steps, not ends. They are steps on a long journey, at the end of which lie Muslim theocratic societies, where *Shari'a* law rules. Freedom of religion, freedom of the press, freedom of speech, and the equality of women and non-believers will be as offensive to Muslims then as guide dogs and alcohol are now. There will be no end to the complaints, demands, concessions and things offensive to the Jihadists until that goal is reached.

Shari'a Law

Just what is *Shari'a* law? It is the path to be followed by all Muslims and non-Muslims under Islamic rule. But, again, there are as many varieties as there are of Islam itself, and enforcement varies from mild to very stringent—think Afghanistan under the Taliban. The Jihadists want to impose a very strict version on us and on all Muslims.

To understand *Shari'a*, you must first understand a few things considered to be part of most Islamic traditions. The first is *uswa hasana*, the recognition of the Prophet Muhammad as the perfect example of conduct for Muslims.[15] Thus the fact that Muhammad held slaves, had sex with slaves, and condoned the rape of captive women (*Those whom your right hands possess*. Sura 4. *Take in marriage those...of your male and female slaves who are honest*. Sura 24.), and had sex with one of his eleven wives, Aisha, when she was nine, according to the *Hadith*,[16] makes that desirable and admirable conduct for Muslims today, according to the fundamental views of the Jihadists.

For example, Article 1041 of the Civil Code of Iran stated that girls can be engaged before the age of nine, and married at nine: "Marriage before puberty (nine full lunar years for girls) is prohibited. Marriage contracted before reaching puberty with the permission of the guardian is valid provided that the interests of the ward are duly observed." (It has supposedly been updated so that a 50 year old man wanting a fourth wife must wait until she is 13.) Ahmad Al-Mu'bi, who officiates at marriages in Saudi Arabia, said in 2008, "The Prophet Muhammad is the model we follow. He took 'Aisha to be his wife when she was 6, but he had sex with her only when she was 9."[17] So if you are shocked by under-age sex and child marriage, remember, it may not be a good idea, but it's okay under the law for Jihadists—*Shari'a* Law! And the law for everyone if they win.

Slavery is still regarded as acceptable by many Jihadist schools of Islamic thought, again, based on the Qur'an and the "perfect" example of Muhammad, "and many of his companions (who) bought, sold, freed, and captured slaves."[18] "The Qur'an includes multiple references to slaves, slave women, slave concubinage, and the freeing of slaves. It accepts the institution of slavery. It may be noted that the word 'abd' (slave) is rarely used, being more commonly replaced by some periphrasis such as ma malakat aymanukum ('that which your right hands own')."[18] Sheik Saleh Al-Fawzan, a leading Saudi Government cleric and author of the country's religious curriculum said, "Slavery is part of jihad, and jihad will remain as long (as) there is Islam."[19] Which is why CNN estimates are that there are currently thousands of slaves held by Muslims in the Sudan.[20] The fundamentalist views of the Jihadists are not out of mainstream Islamic thought, despite wishful thinking on the part of many academics—they are a major branch of Islam.

You also need to understand that most Islamic scholars consider the *Hadith*, the traditions of the Prophet and his companions, necessary for determining the *Sunna*, or Muslim way of life and for understanding Allah's commands in the *Qur'an*. (*Sunna* is also sometimes used in place of *Hadith*, which can be confusing). The *Hadith* have almost the religious weight of the *Qur'an*, but some are considered strong and others weak. Considered especially strong are the *Hadith* collections labeled *Sahih Bukhari* and *Sahih Muslim*. Most Muslims consider the *Hadith* to be the words, actions and stories of Muhammad, not of Allah. The *Hadith,* like the *Qur'an,* were written down long after Muhammad's death.

Woman under *Shari'a*

Under many of the versions of *Shari'a,* based on the *Qur'an* and the *Hadith,* in many Islamic countries:

- A woman's testimony is worth only half of a man's.[21]
- A woman may only inherit half of what a man may.[21]
- A man may beat his wife for disobedience.[21]
- A man may marry up to four women, a woman may marry only one man. Men are also permitted concubines and female slaves.[21]
- A man may divorce any of his wives at a word, leaving them destitute. A woman may not divorce a man unless he agrees and divorces her.[21]
- A Muslim man may marry a non-Muslim. A Muslim woman may not.[21]
- Women must cover their heads, or their entire bodies, and may not have contact with a man outside her family.[21]
- A woman must have four male Muslim witnesses to prove rape. Lacking four witnesses, a rape victim can be found guilty of adultery and stoned to death. "On October 30, 2008, the United Nations condemned the stoning to death of Aisha Duhulowa, a 13-year-old girl who had been gang-raped and then sentenced to death by a Sharia court for fornication (Zina). She was screaming and begging for mercy, but when some family members attempted to intervene, shots were fired by the Islamic militia and a baby was killed."[22]
- A wife must have sex whenever a husband wishes—there is no marital rape under *Shari'a.*[23]

This is *Shari'a.*

Other aspects of *Shari'a* Law

If the discriminatory treatment of women and girls were not enough of a concern under *Shari'a,* it has many other aspects that are in direct conflict with freedom and Western civilization, where they have been fully implemented. *Shari'a* Law envisions no separation of Mosque and state—the religion of Islam is the government. A Muslim is enjoined not to obey secular law if it conflicts with *Shari'a.*[24] It is a religious law, and seeks to implement the religious injunctions given to Mohammad by Allah over 1,300 years ago. We should note that if Christian law from the seventh century were to be imposed on modern society, the effect on freedom would be as devastating. Civilization has evolved, but *Shari'a* Law in the form the Jihadists are determined to impose has not.

Under *Shari'a*, a Muslim who leaves Islam, or anyone who commits blasphemy by criticizing Islam or the Prophet may be punished with death.[25] Recently in Pakistan, "A Christian serving a life sentence in Karachi Central Jail on accusations that he had sent text messages blaspheming the prophet of Islam died ... amid suspicions that he was murdered."[26] The only Christian in Pakistan's cabinet criticized the blasphemy law, and was murdered.[27] A month earlier, "Lawyers showered the suspected killer of a prominent Pakistani governor with rose petals when he arrived at court Wednesday, and an influential Muslim scholars group praised the assassination of the outspoken opponent of laws that order death for those who insult Islam."[28] This is *Shari'a*.

An important concept of *Shari'a* Law is that of *Dhimmi* (The plural is often rendered dhimmis, dhimma or dhimmia.) *Dhimmis* are the "People of the Book," mainly Christians and Jews, whom Muslims say are protected people under Islamic rule as long as they pay the poll tax. Critics say *dhimmis* are subservient peoples, with a status like African Americans had under the Jim Crow laws. "After the jihad concludes in a given area with the conquest of infidel territory, the dhimma, or treaty of protection, may be granted to the conquered 'People of the Book'—historically, Jews, Christians, and Zoroastrians. The dhimma provides that the life and property of the infidel are exempted from jihad for as long as the Muslim rulers permit, which has generally meant for as long as the subject non-Muslims—the dhimmi—prove economically useful to the Islamic state. The Quran spells out the payment of the jizya (poll-tax or head-tax; Sura 9:29), which is the most conspicuous means by which the Muslim overlords exploit the dhimmi. But the jizya is not merely economic in its function; it exists also to humiliate the dhimmi and impress on him the superiority of Islam."[29] In some interpretations, "Islamic law (*Sharia*) forbids dhimmis to build new houses of worship or repair old ones."[30]

And many Muslim scholars defend the execution of gays. "'Under Islamic law is it punishable by death if you are a homosexual?' Binhazim said, 'Yes. It is punishable by death.'"[31] If you do a web search for the keywords "Hanging" and "Gays," you will see shocking photos. Though they are usually smart enough not to allow photographs.

All this is also *Shari'a*. Are there Muslims who believe in updating *Shari'a*, or in not enforcing the extreme versions? Of course. But in Muslim countries and Muslim communities around the world, for many decades now, the trend has been towards the fundamentalist version, the Salafist view of the original, or "pure," Islam. And the secular, moderate Muslims who disagreed often pay with their lives as apostates.

Can the West Survive?

In his book *America Alone*, Mark Steyn suggests that Europe and probably Canada are already lost to radical Islam, due to the iron hand of demographics. Steyn says that in many European countries and in Canada, the birth rate among the native population has fallen so far below the replacement rate of 2.1

live births per woman, that it is unlikely the native population will recover. The United States has a birth rate of 2.1, but would not without Hispanic immigrants. You can find much on the Net, touting or disputing the demographic problem, proving again, I suppose that "figures don't lie, but liars figure."

In 2006, Muammar al-Gaddafi said, "There are signs that Allah will grant Islam victory in Europe without swords, without guns, without military conquests. The 50 million Muslims of Europe will turn it into a Muslim continent within a few decades." [32] Others dismiss the "Eurabia" concept.

But you cannot dismiss the growing danger and violence in some areas of Europe. Jews are abandoning Malmo, Sweden due to Muslim hate crimes.[33] It is reported that there are over 750 Muslim "no-go" zones in France where the government is no longer in control, and where police, fire and doctors often dare-not enter.[34]

"In Australia, Norway, Sweden and other Western nations, there is a distinct race-based crime ... being ignored by the diversity police: Islamic men are raping Western women for ethnic reasons. We know this because the rapists have openly declared their sectarian motivations ... In France, in the banlieues, where gang rape is now known simply as tournantes or 'pass-around,' victims know the police will not protect them." [35] But it's also a cultural attack. Muslim women who are perceived as acting Western or immodest are also often victims.[36]

Europe's response to Jihadist violence and threats has been to try to restrict freedom of speech, hoping that by not criticizing the Jihadists, they can prevent violence. There is no First Amendment in Europe or Canada, and even truth is no defense to a charge of "hate speech" claimed by offended Muslims. Review the court cases against Elisabeth Sabaditsch-Wolff in Austria,[37] Shane Overton in the UK,[38] Lars Hedegaard in Denmark,[39] Geert Wilders[40] and Gregorius Nekschot[41] in the Netherlands, Michel Houellebecq in France[42] or of Ezra Levant and Mark Steyn in Canada.[43] (Levant and Steyn have detailed their cases in books that are worth reading. See the Chapter References.) Even when the defendants were acquitted, the costs of the case and the negative publicity, which can destroy reputations and make your family a target for the violent jihadists, have a chilling effect on free speech and the discussion.

Europe has its own illegal immigrant problem,[44] and the rot is everywhere. In a painful column entitled, "A stranger in my own land," a British priest's wife writes, "For four years, we lived in inner-city Birmingham, in what has been a police no-go area for 20 years ... When we arrived, the population was predominantly Pakistani. Now Somalis are there in equal number. Most of the run-down Irish pubs were turned into mosques during our time ... our doctors and nurses drive in from afar, the police, as mentioned before, have shut down their stations and never venture in unless in extremis — they and ambulance crews have been known to be attacked — even the local Imam lives in a leafier area." [45] That she felt the need to write anonymously is hardly surprising.

Given the falling native birthrates that will make sustaining the European and Canadian welfare states impossible, plus the growth of a Muslim population and increased radicalism, I believe that Mark Steyn is right. America will stand alone to defend Western civilization in twenty years. It is not clear we will be up to the challenge, or that we will not have knuckled under to the Jihad long before then.

The Next Terrorist Attack on America

Nothing seems surer to me than that the violent wing of the Jihadists will eventually launch another major attack on the United States. Below is one possible scenario, neither the worst, nor that hard to carry out.

Twenty-four well-trained, fanatical young men, Jihadists from Muslim countries, set out for Mexico, where their appearance allows them to blend in. They meet pre-arranged contacts among the ruthless Mexican drug cartels, which have been well-paid in advance with funds from the oil-producing Muslim countries, grown rich with American dollars since Americans cannot drill for oil here, or substitute nuclear power, due to political restraints.

The cartels, who will do quite literally anything for money, have agreed to smuggle them into the United States. It is, in fact, easier and cheaper than smuggling in the automatic weapons, hand grenades and C-4 explosive that are already waiting for them.

The men are smuggled in, by different cartels using different routes, in teams of four. Twenty get through to marry up with the weapons and explosives. The four who are apprehended, in a bit of rare bad luck for the smugglers given our unsecure borders, have cover stories ready. They have fake IDs, are unarmed and not carrying drugs. They claim they are fleeing Islamic extremism to build a new life of freedom in the United States. In a rare show of fortitude by the government, they are deported to the countries on their false IDs, despite the protests of CAIR and various professional leftist America-bashers.

The five successful teams are delivered to their pre-smuggled weapon catches and to cars already provided for them. They disperse across the country, driving carefully and obeying all speed laws. Police would be unlikely to stop them in any case, fearful of being accused of "profiling."

Once in place, one by one they check in by e-mail with a pre-arranged code, "1453" to a cut-out contact, who relays it to bin Laden's replacement through a secure network. An American security agent intercepts the e-mail due to the foreign destination, but "1453," the year Constantinople fell to an earlier Muslim Jihad, means nothing to him.[46]

There they wait, keeping a lower profile than the 9/11 attackers, worried that Americans will be more alert now. They have nothing to fear on that score.

Finally the message "Mehmed" comes back to their new Yahoo e-mail accounts. Again, it has meaning only to them. At a planned time, all five teams move against their pre-selected targets.

Team one, trained to drive 18-wheelers, moves first, at 4:00 am, seizing two gasoline trucks with sleeping, unarmed drivers at a truck stop near a large, west-coast city. They kill the drivers, but keep the bodies in the trucks, which they drive to a large bridge leading into the city. At 7:30 am Pacific Time, they drive onto the bridge half a bridge length apart, stop the trucks as though broken down, and set explosive timers for ten minutes. They then begin shooting drivers and passengers on either end of the bridge, creating panic. The first police car arrives just as the fuel tankers explode. People caught between the two conflagrations begin diving into the river, to their deaths. The bridge will be unusable for six months, but thankfully does not collapse as the terrorists hoped.

At the same time, Team Two seizes a rural elementary school in a Midwestern county without a SWAT team. After killing three adults and a boy caught in the cross fire, they herd the teachers and students into the gym for better control. Cell phones are seized, and phone wires cut. Explosives are planted around the gym so that they can be easily detonated to kill most of the 430 students and teachers.

All black students and teachers are released and told to "run for their lives," in hopes of aggravating America's racial tensions. A black teacher is given a message: All American troops in Afghanistan must immediately surrender to the Taliban to face justice for crimes against Muslims and Islam. They will shoot one child every ten minutes until they are notified by the Taliban by satellite radio of the surrender. The first child, an 8-year-old girl, is taken to the front steps and shot to death exactly ten minutes later.

Twenty-two children have been murdered by the time the state police SWAT team storms the building. Only 43 badly injured children and three teachers survive the explosion. Eight cops are killed as well as all four terrorists.

Team Three seizes a Jewish Community Center in Florida. They demand Israel release all "political prisoners," and begin shooting a hostage every five minutes, aware that SWAT teams are likely to react faster in this location. They have only killed nine before the police assault. The explosion kills 143 people, plus three of the terrorists and two cops.

Team Four seizes an office building in New England. Team Five seizes a Casino, a fine symbol of western decadence with gambling, alcohol and indecently covered women, all *haraam* (forbidden) under *Shari'a* law.

By the end of the day, 2,122 Americans in five locations are dead, as are 18 of the terrorists. The two in custody are wounded and have been provided with ACLU lawyers to protect their "Constitutional rights." Vigilantes are attacking innocent Muslims in the streets, but also Hindus and Sikhs, unable to distinguish between them. There are an additional 60 or so murders of innocent people by angry mobs. A run on gun shops develops, and many are sold out by day's end. Blacks riot in two cities when white gun shop owners refuse to sell to them, burning the shops and surrounding areas, prompting more panic.

Al Jazeera play a tape from al Qaeda announcing that "the first wave" has attacked "the Great Satan," and that more waves will follow. The stock market goes into free fall, and closes. Experts predict a loss of 3,000 points on the Dow when it re-opens. China and other foreign countries announce they will no longer buy U.S. bonds, "Until we see if the U.S. will collapse." This produces a financial panic that makes 2008 look like a mild setback. Businesses and organizations cancel all meetings and 95% of orders of products, creating an instant deep recession on top of the country's economic troubles. The cost far exceeds the estimated $2 trillion cost of the 9/11 attacks.[47] The cost to the Jihadists is 20 martyrs and perhaps $10 million. Tops.

Since black hostages were spared at the school and two other locations, white racists are claiming militant blacks colluded with the terrorists, and that the terrorists spared blacks because our black President was born a Muslim.

The President goes on TV and borrowing from Bill Clinton, promises to "bring those responsible to justice." He also announces that he has authorized the CIA, other agencies and the military to use "all measures they believe appropriate" to develop information about the perpetrators and to prevent future attacks. There is no dissent from politicians of either party, but 143 CIA agents resign, realizing a future administration might prosecute them for following the President's orders. The Chairman of the Joint Chiefs announces that "under no conditions" will he order troops to use any coercive techniques to gather information on terrorists, because they might be punished in the future for doing so. The heads of the other services back him, and all are relieved by the President, only to discover that no general or admiral will take the job. There is a wave of resignations and retirements of military officers, creating further panic in a public aware that the country is descending into chaos, depression, and a collapse of morale in the armed services.

When a bi-partisan group of legislators, responding to public demand, announces impeachment hearings, riots break out in the largest cities, with thousands of deaths and billions of dollars more in damages. Martial Law is declared in a dozen cities where gang rule has replaced the local governments. The military is sent in to quell the disturbances.

And thus the Republic descends into the abyss.

Can it happen? Why not? Could it be this bad? Now that the Obama Administration has tacitly accepted a nuclear-armed Iran[48], it could, in fact, be much, much worse.

I may, of course, just be a paranoid alarmist. In fact, some folks said so when I published a column, mentioned in the *Introduction*, entitled, "American's War on Terror will be Long, Slow and Cruel," in the *Courier Post*. In that essay, I wrote, "A man with a wild look in his eye, a pipeline to his god, and a weapon in his hand has ever been a danger. But the weapons now are explosives powerful enough to destroy buildings, snuffing out hundreds of lives. Soon they will be gasses that can slaughter thousands, diseases that can kill millions. Perhaps even atomic bombs. And men like Osama bin Laden and Saddam Hussein will use them without compunction. They believe they can humble America by breaking our will to resist." That column was published on August 28, 1998, three years before the 9/11 attacks. For all the good it did.

If the scenario above isn't scary enough, imagine this. Suppose the Jihadists solve the admittedly difficult problems of creating (or buying) and transporting nuclear weapons, and there are atomic detonations in New York and Los Angeles, those being good targets with lots of uninspected cargo coming in. Upwards of five million Americans are dead. Many more are sick and dying. The economy is virtually gone and we face starvation and poverty for everyone. On the plus side, we didn't water board anyone to try to prevent it, so our leadership feels really good about themselves.

Given that the Jihadists are non-state actors, we don't know what country to strike back at with our nukes, if we had the courage to do so, and no assurance that by doing so we are not incinerating millions more innocents. Did they get them from Iran? North Korea? Pakistan? Russia via criminal gangs? Or elsewhere? The Jihadist demands are simple. Withdraw all American forces to the homeland, disband the American military and institute *Shari'a* law. Or more American cities will die.

What now, Mr. President? (Assuming of course that Washington wasn't one of the targets and we *have* a president.)

Let's turn from the contemplation of the unbearable to a bright spot in the struggle with the Twin Jihads.

Moderate Muslims

There is a bitter joke that a moderate Muslim is one who is out of ammo and needs to reload. That's grossly unfair, but it grows out of fear, because to outside observers, it appears impossible to pick out the seemingly ordinary Muslim who suddenly "goes Jihad" and murders people from the peaceful majority. Even Muslims in the new Jihadist's family are often stunned. The classic case, of course, is the New York Muslim who started a TV station to showcase how "moderate" most Muslims were—and then beheaded his wife because she threatened to leave him.[49]

Even when non-Muslims suspect that a formerly "moderate" Muslim has been radicalized, as with Army Major Nidal Hasan, who murdered 13 fellow soldiers, they fear to say anything, for fear of being labeled "Islamophobic," a possible career-ending charge.[50] Political Correctness kills.

It's also hard to characterize many Muslims in the world as "moderate," given what we can know of their beliefs, even if they are not at a given time engaging in Jihad, violent or otherwise. The mainstream media praised the people of Egypt in their struggle for democracy. But since a Pew poll found that 82% of Egyptians favor stoning adulterers to death and 84% favor executing people who leave Islam for another religion,[51] their view of democratic freedoms may be somewhat different than ours. The full report on the poll, listed in the *Chapter References*, is worth reading. There are bright spots, but it also suggests that fundamentalists and Islamic supremacists constitute a far larger percentage of Muslims than that "tiny minority" we so often hear about.

And, indeed, some argue there is no distinction in Islam between moderates and radicals. "One doesn't need to be a student of Islam to know that neither within the Quran nor the tradition from which it springs and which it in turn

43

continues to shape is there any warrant for, say, the distinction between 'radical Islam' and 'moderate Islam' that Peter King and legions of others uncritically endorse. Though it is not intended as such, a genuinely devout Muslim will regard as offensive the suggestion that his religiosity is moderate." [52]

But, clearly, there are secular Muslims, which is perhaps a better term than moderate. Some may be very devout, others more of the "Christmas and Easter" type of commitment found among many Christians. The great distinction is that secular Muslims do not wish to impose Islam and *Shari'a* law on each other or on non-Muslims, or live in a state where the Islamic religious authorities are also the political authorities.

If the Jihadists are, as I believe, hundreds of times more numerous than apologists and Jihad-deniers on the Left believe, there are far more secular Muslims than many critics of Islam would admit. There would be many more, but it takes a special courage to stand up to thugs with guns ready to kill you for any deviation from what they see as the true path, when you are armed with only words and sweet reason.

Below are listed some of these secular Muslims and former Muslims. They are people of great courage. We must cherish, aid and, as best we can, help protect them. Nor can we let their voices be lost. They are fighting our fight, but equally important, the fight of the hundreds of fellow Muslims slaughtered by Jihadists every month.

No to Political Islam is a coalition of secular Muslim groups advocating for human rights within Islam. Their website says, "The *Sharia* should be opposed for its imposition of theocracy over democracy, its abuse of human rights, its institutionalized discrimination, its denial of human dignity and individual autonomy, its punishment of alternative lifestyle choices, and for the severity of its punishments." [53] Their website is listed in the Chapter References, and is worth reading. You know that by supporting reform, they are on someone's target list.

Walid Shoebat describes himself as a former terrorist. "This was in the early 1980s when I was being trained for Jihad activities in the USA along with many other young foreign students and U.S. citizens. The Imams are the prime recruiters for terrorism then as they are still today." [54] Having left Islam marks him for death. His statements as a former Muslim are far stronger than anything someone like Glenn Beck says.

Dr. Zuhdi Jasser, a Sunni Muslim and former Navy Lt. Commander, is president of the American Islamic Forum for Democracy. "'Of the last 220 arrests by the US Department of Justice on terror charges, Jasser notes, more than 180 of the suspects were Muslims. You have 1.5 percent of the population that is over 80% of the arrests,' he says. 'And the arc has been increasing.' Rather than remain on the defensive, Jasser says, the US and the West at large must take a muscular, offensive approach toward promoting the ideals of liberalism. Those who say democracy and political Islam can peacefully coexist, he says, are ill-informed." [55]

Asra Nomani writes with courage and clarity about the problem of radicalization in the Muslim American community. "We have seen the encroachment of extremist interpretations of Islam into our American Muslim community, and as a community we have largely sat on the fence about these very serious issues ... Starting in the 1970s, I saw puritanical, intolerant ideologies creep into my community. I also watched as many moderate Muslims simply cowered or walked away, intimidated into thinking they were less pious or faithful—or concluding it wasn't worth the bother."[56] I urge you to follow her columns and articles.

Hasan Mahmud writes in *Front Page Magazine*, "The litmus test to differentiate a progressive Muslim from a radical one is to inquire about the belief in *Sharia* law being divine. *Sharia* law is by no means a benign legal system; to the contrary, it is a malignant weapon that aids the pursuit of a global theocracy. The claim that the violence of *Sharia* law is Allah's Law destroys the legitimacy of Islam as a 'Religion of Peace.' Like many Muslims I am deeply concerned with the alarming penetration of the institution of *Sharia* law into the West ... Muslim women are its primary victims, followed by secular Muslims and non-Muslims."[57] Again, you need to read the whole article.

Tawfik Hamid is a scholar and author from Egypt. He writes, " ... our current Islamic teaching creates violence and hatred toward Non-Muslims. We Muslims are the ones who need to change. Until now we have accepted polygamy, the beating of women by men, and killing those who convert from Islam to other religions. We have never had a clear and strong stand against the concept of slavery or wars, to spread our religion and to subjugate others to Islam and force them to pay a humiliating tax called Jizia. We ask others to respect our religion while all the time we curse non-Muslims loudly (in Arabic) in our Friday prayers in the Mosques."[58]

Waseem Sayed, spokesperson for the Ahmadiyya Muslim Community in the US, says, " ... there are negative influences being exerted — upon especially the Muslim youth in the United States — by people like al Awlaki on the Internet ... If we just sit by, more and more these extremists will take hold the banner of Islam and say this is what Islam is."[59] Ahmadiyya Muslims are persecuted in many Muslim lands for holding less than orthodox beliefs.

There are blogs on the Internet by *Women Against Sharia*[60] and *Muslims Against Sharia*[61] but they do not list who is behind them. Could be non-Muslims opposing Islam, I suppose. Could be secular Muslims who fear their co-religionists. In any case, they post interesting articles.

Muslims for Progressive Values,[62] on the other hand, is a brave and open organization that lists its worldwide leadership. Unfortunately, our leadership is often too busy placating extremist groups to support these secular Muslims. "White House officials are boosting the visibility and clout of Islamic revivalist groups in the United States, and are sidelining the growing network of liberal-minded, modern American Muslims."[63]

Fear of retaliation against secular Muslims is certainly legitimate in Muslim majority countries. "Gunmen shot and killed a Muslim cleric highly critical of a hardline Islamist sect, in an attack outside his home in Maiduguri, northeast

Nigeria, witnesses said."[64]

"A bomb exploded at the headquarters of a moderate Islamic group in the Indonesian capital Jakarta on Tuesday, wounding four people including a police officer whose hand was blown off. The device was in a package sent to the office of the Liberal Islam Network (JIL), a grouping of religious intellectuals ..."[65]

Yes, there are large numbers of moderate or secular Muslims. When you wonder why they don't speak up, it's because when they do, they put their lives at risk. *Ayaan Hirsi Ali* suffered genital mutilation as a child, fled a forced marriage to the Netherlands, became a member of the Dutch parliament, and made a film with Theo van Gogh, *Submission*, about the treatment of women in traditional Islam. For which van Gogh was murdered on the street by a Muslim and Hirsi Ali was forced into hiding. Her book, *Infidel*, is well worth reading. How many non-Muslims are speaking up for these threatened, secular Muslims?

Many Muslims are, but their voices are often lost.[67] Islam and America need more of these courageous, secular Muslims, not fewer. And that will only happen if we do not lump them with the Jihadists. And if we offer them support.

Islamophobia was not created by Danish cartoonists. It springs from 9/11 and the thousands of attacks and murders in the name of Jihad, Islam and Allah that have taken place since that awful day.[68]

Islamophobia is not caused by a Congressman holding hearings on radicalization. It is caused when terrorists cut the throats of small children, including a baby, in the name of Allah and fellow Muslims celebrate by passing out candy in the streets.[69]

And it is not Islamophobia that kills Muslims. It is Jihadism that slaughters them by the thousands, at the hands of co-religionists and the hands of those they attack who defend themselves, causing innocent deaths, as war always does. "Muslims comprised 85% of al-Qaeda's victims from 2004 to 2008 ... FBI hate crime statistics, spanning 1996 to 2009, record not even a single Muslim dying due to an anti-Islamic incident in the United States."[70]

And it is not cartoonists or Congressmen who defame Islam, but child murderers acting in the name of Allah.

I have left out the horrors of honor killings of female relatives or of the genital mutilation of young girls, because, though wide spread in Islamic cultures, they are not limited to them, and the Islamic mandate for them is disputed. But it is worth doing an Internet search for "honor killing" and "female genital mutilation" to learn more about these horrors, the large percentage of them that are carried out by Muslims, how fundamental Islam supports them and why we must fight these barbaric practices as well.

Those who would excuse the murders of the Jihadists on the grounds that the crusades perpetrated evil on Muslims 700 to 900 years ago should remember that Islam spread through conquering—none too gently—Christian lands, including Spain and Constantinople, and were only turned back from conquering all of Europe by European victories at Tours in 732[71] (before the First Crusade!) at the Sieges of Vienna in both 1529[72] and 1683,[73] and the Battle of Lepanto in 1571[74] (where upwards of 15,000 Christian galley slaves were freed).

We are in a long, two-front war with the Jihadists. One front is a PR, political and propaganda war, the "Stealth Jihad." The other front is a violent, asymmetrical insurgency war, the hardest type to fight. It is made all the more difficult in that the violent Jihadists do not have a head we can cut off, but appear in thousands of variations, from the laughable to the incredibly deadly. It will not end in our lifetimes—unless we lose.

And if we lose, the world's 1.3 billion Muslims will suffer as badly, perhaps worse, than those of us of other faiths, or no faith, will suffer. We are fighting the Jihad for the majority of Muslims, too.

We are constrained in fighting this war by a lack of will, a lack of understanding and a lack of faith among not only the general population, but among too many of our leaders. We are constrained in fighting this war by the financial and immigration problems detailed in earlier chapters. We are constrained in fighting this war because our allies may be forced into neutrality, ultimately to support the Jihadists, as they develop large Islamist populations.

And we are constrained in fighting this war because in addition to fighting an insurgent war, our military must also be configured for a conventional war, facing a new power rising in the East.

Chapter Five: China—Does the Dragon Awake?

I know it's a cliché, but there's a rule that you aren't allowed to write about China without using a dragon metaphor. In this case, I also use a question mark, as I think the rise of China is less an existential threat to the Republic than our other challenges, because of a number of mitigating factors. But it is still a threat.

I'll avoid provoking additional racism charges by not using "Yellow Peril," the racist scare tactic from the days when Chinese immigrants and workers were treated worse, in many cases, than black slaves in the South, the Chinese being economically cheaper to replace when they died of privation and over-work. But there is little modern comment or demands for "reparations" to be paid to the descendents of these abused Chinese laborers. We have forgotten—or never learned—about this blot on American history, which included riots and murder. But, trust me, China has not forgotten.

The rise of China is enough of a threat that it complicates and weakens our ability to deal with the other three crises I listed above. It is a threat that we must respond to. And it's a threat that can produce devastating fiscal consequences for our economy.

I do not think that the "Red Chinese" want to conquer the world, or the United States. I don't think they expect to lead a Marxist revolution that will make Communists of the everyone. I'm not sure, given the success of their state-market system in building their economy, they even believe all that much in Marxism anymore.[1]

I do believe that the Middle Kingdom wants to be a major military and economic power. I think that the current Chinese Communist Party is seen as having the "Mandate of Heaven"[2] and the leadership will continue to nod toward socialism, while behaving increasingly like a traditional, oppressive Chinese dynasty pursuing traditional Chinese foreign policy goals.[3] These goals will include protecting China by absorbing surrounding nations into the empire[4] or, when that's not practical, by making them client states.

High on the list is bringing the holdout of *Kuomintang*[5] power, Taiwan, under control of the central government as it has Tibet[6], despite a bloody resistance there. Hong Kong has also been brought into the empire, though with some limited political and economic freedom because that status has proved useful to China. North Korea and Mongolia are, of course, already client states of China.

Communist Vietnam was a client during the war against America, which they won after the U.S. Congress cut off promised aid to our ally, the Republic of Vietnam. Vietnam has its own client states in Laos and Cambodia, but has a traditional distrust of China, and has begun building military relationships with the U.S. to counter China's growing power.[7]

Taiwan has held out only because our fleet protects it. Tibet went under because no other nation could project power deep into Asia to keep it free of Chinese rule. Thousands of "Free Tibet" bumper stickers on U.S. college campuses have proven no match for a couple of divisions of infantry.

China's Goals

This is my opinion. Take it for what it's worth. I believe China's goals are to:

1. Become a first rate economic and military power such that no nation will challenge her militarily unless China presents an existential threat, which she won't. Thus it wants to be able to back down the United States over Asian issues, because a war would do us more damage than conceding small steps, one by one.

2. Make Taiwan a political part of China. Taiwan's status at first would probably have a degree of economic freedom, more like Hong Kong than Tibet, because that would be useful to China economically. Because Taiwan is an island, it could be quarantined, to prevent the political contamination of the masses on the mainland.

3. Make the western Pacific, the China Seas and perhaps part of the Indian Ocean a "Chinese Lake," where China's navy is mostly unchallenged and trade is at China's pleasure.

4. Bring Japan, Korea and Southeast Asia first into a position of neutrality, then under Chinese dominance economically and politically as quasi-client states. This is a project that will take decades, but the Chinese are more patient than we are, and think further into the future.

With the above accomplished, China, not the United States, will be the world's "superpower," a power it will use much more in China's interests than we use our power in US interests. (No word yet if they will call it the "Greater East Asia Co-Prosperity Sphere.") And we may not be able to do much about it, given the other claims on our declining resources. "The force driving the rise of the East is exactly the same as the force that drove the earlier rise of the West: the interaction of geography with economics and technology." [8]

China's military buildup

American ability to project power and protect trade by controlling the seas is in decline, and the fiscal crisis makes reversing it unlikely at best. "Because 95% and 90% respectively of U.S. and world foreign trade moves by sea, maritime interdiction is the quickest route to both the strangulation of any given nation and chaos in the international system. First Britain and then the U.S. have been the guarantors of the open oceans. The nature of this task demands a large blue-water fleet that simply cannot be abridged." [9] But, "We have the smallest navy in almost a century, declining in the past 50 years to 286 from 1,000 principal combatants." [9] And further cuts are planned.

Meanwhile, "China is deploying new submarines at an impressive rate—three a year. They are suited to pushing back U.S. power projection in the Western

Pacific. China's much-discussed ballistic and cruise missiles also seem designed to keep U.S. surface forces far from China's soil. And China seems increasingly inclined to define the oceans off its shores as extensions of the shores—territory to be owned and controlled like 'blue national soil.' This concept is incompatible with the idea of the oceans as a 'common.'"[10]

With the Pentagon cutting back on the U.S. F-22 Stealth Fighter, China has reportedly launched its own stealth fighter, the J-20[11], and "disclosed that a long-awaited Chinese anti-ship missile, designed to sink an American aircraft carrier, was nearly operational."[12]

China is also building an aircraft carrier. Can one carrier stand up to the 11 in the American fleet—or however many are left after budget cuts? No. But our carriers may be involved elsewhere, or mothballed. "China has a nuclear arsenal and the world's second-largest defence budget after the United States—although experts believe China spends more than it reveals—but its military capabilities beyond its borders are limited. As a tool for projecting power, the aircraft carrier is unsurpassed."[13] The point of a Chinese carrier is power projection. And do we know how many carriers China will have in ten years—or how many we will have? A 12% increase in Chinese defense spending,[14] or a Chinese deep water carrier fleet may not be enough to defeat the United States in a conventional war now. But China's military capability is growing, while ours is shrinking. The point is not to defeat us, but to make fighting more expensive than submitting to their demands. Sun Tzu was, after all, Chinese.

China is also developing cyber war capability. The "Red Hacker Alliance, a Beijing-sanctioned 'network security' organization ... reportedly has over 300,000 members and paid staff that includes university-trained computer science experts. It undertakes 'patriotic' cyberhacking as well as various 'government-sponsored' projects."[15] China is also interested in space-based systems that can "burn ships" and disrupt command and control systems.[16] Meanwhile, the U.S. is cutting back on space development due to the budget crisis.

In a decade, it may be more prudent for an American president to concede to small demands from China a step at a time, rather than fight a conventional war that is very expensive and very bloody, over, say Taiwan's autonomy. Especially when the factors covered in earlier chapters are debilitating the United States. Would you send your son or daughter to die to keep Taiwan or even Japan from becoming Chinese client states?

China's Economic Power

It is, of course, China's growing economy that allows it to grow its military muscle. China is now the world's second largest economy, behind the US and ahead of Japan.[17] If a weakened America was forced to allow China to dominate Japan, South Korea, Taiwan, Southeast Asia and even perhaps India, the economic power of this Asian coalition would be formidable indeed.

China now emits 24% of the world's carbon dixoide, and its emissions, growing at 10% a year, far exceed that of the United States and will soon exceed the entire Western hemisphere.[17] This not only highlights China's growing industrial might, but makes moot environmentalists' efforts to ruin our economy through "Cap and Trade" schemes to reduce carbon output.

And China feels no need to play by the rules. "They're stealing our technology, violating all sorts of patent-protection laws, hacking into Google and infringing on intellectual-property rights. In fact, 80 percent of Chinese software is reportedly pirated from American companies." [11] The Chinese government sponsors industrial espionage to build their economy.[19]

And to power that economy, they have, "initiated a research and development project in thorium molten-salt (nuclear) reactor technology." [20]

China also controls 95% of the world's rare earth elements (REE), which are "essential for a diverse and expanding array of high-technology applications, including the magnets, metal alloys, and batteries for key defense systems, as well as many current and emerging alternative energy technologies." [21] We'd better develop our own sources or stockpile some before the shooting starts!

"China is investing in all forms of transportation...(and) has built a national expressway network larger than the one that connects the European Union and almost equivalent of the US Interstate Highway System....In 2009, 166 airports were open to civilian transportation. This number is expected to increase to 260 by 2015." [22]

The upshot of China's economic growth is that they own a large part of our burgeoning national debt, second only to our own Federal Reserve Bank. Debt, too, can be used as a weapon. "We're talking about China dumping some $68 billion in US debt in just one year. Indeed, it is clear China is making moves to continue its ascent to super power status, removing any potential weakness it might face in future conflict with the US (such as overreliance on the US as a trade partner or reserve currency)." [23]

There are arguments against China as a threat

China remains a major trading partner, selling the U.S. $365 billion in goods each year. It is also the third largest importer of U.S. goods.[24] But trading partners have gone to war before.[25]

China also has great problems. "China has 700 million very poor people. By 2050, it will have 400 million very old people. It will 'get old before it gets rich,' as conservative writer Mark Steyn likes to say." [26] And as is typical of Communist countries, the destruction of the environment may derail their economic growth.[27]

And China's one-child policy, a traditional Asian preference for sons, the availability of abortion and ultrasound and, certainly, the age-old horror of infanticide (or "full-birth abortion" if you prefer) means that, "By the year 2020, there will be 30 million more men than women of marriageable age in this giant empire."[28] While that demographic disaster will weaken China, it will also make large infantry losses rather acceptable to the Chinese leadership.

China has a huge inflation problem as well that is going to create unrest, economic disruption and political trouble.[29] And it's quite possible that China will crumble like the Soviet Union, in the face of all these problems. "China is a powder keg that could explode at any moment. And if it does explode, chaos could ensue — as the Chinese are only too well aware, the country has a brutal history of carnage at the hands of unruly mobs."[29]

Of course, if a collapse in the Eurozone or the U.S. fiscal house of cards—or both—pulls the world's economy into a major depression, China will follow us into the abyss, given how interlocked the global economy is.

My best guess is that China is perhaps less likely to implode than we are, given the government's power over its citizens. China's major weaknesses may make it less formidable than many fear, but that it will be enough of a challenge militarily and economically that it will help accelerate a collapse in America. Ironically, a complete American collapse would be economically disastrous for China as well. They may want to dominate Asia and international trade, but they need America to be viable, if only as a second-class power buying their goods. We are rivals who, nonetheless, are propping each other up in some ways.

Much will depend on how these cards play out. If they play out wrong, your children and grandchildren—those who survive—will be living in a very different, much poorer and certainly far less free world.

So, to see what that world might be, let's look at ...

Chapter Six: What Will a Collapse Look Like?

We are treading into the realm of futuristic fiction. And there are multiple possible scenarios, none good. I suspect the best-case scenario is that the country muddles through, but with a lot more financial, political and physical pain than most folks now expect.

A second, not at all far fetched possibility is that the Jihadists are able to obtain or develop one or more nuclear devices. Delivery would not be that hard, with thousands of unexamined cargo containers coming into our ports every day. Jihadists willing to die murdering a million *kuffer* for Allah would be eager to volunteer. Nor would it be difficult to bring them together with the bombs, concealed in containers in a U.S. port, or to teach them to detonate them.

The results of the nuclear destruction of New York, Washington DC, Los Angeles or perhaps all three would go far beyond the millions of dead and dying. The economy would drop to a level last seen in the 1890s. People dependent on modern technology or medicine would simple have no alternative to death. Millions of service, management and creative jobs would vanish. People with skills such as basic nursing, carpentry, small crop farming and hunting would be in the best shape. Control would break down. Gangs would pray on the non-violent and vulnerable. Financial assets like 401Ks and saving accounts would be worthless, but firearms, ammo, hand tools and food would be immensely valuable. There would be military rule, of necessity, in many areas, if we had enough forces left. There would suddenly be a 98% majority demanding increased security over any aspects of civil liberties. The imagined hate crimes against Muslims the mainstream media likes to speculate over now would become a terrible reality. America the affluent would vanish in favor of America the subsistent. The barter economy—or the violent economy—would rule.

Caliphate, a frightening novel by Tom Kratman, a retired Army LtCol turned best-selling science fiction novelist, depicts one such possible future.[1] As scary as it is, it is rosier than my view of our country after a nuke strike.

But I think a gradual deterioration will be even more likely. The terrifying results I suggest for a nuclear strike will still happen, just more slowly. The collapse has already started, and will pick up speed, especially once the tipping point, beyond which recovery is not possible, is reached. Certainly, as we weaken, a major conventional terror attack, along the lines of the scenario I presented in *Chapter Four*, will become more likely. Jihadists will not hesitate to help push the Great Satan over the edge.

Here's what I expect we may see, in part or in whole, not necessarily in this order:

- Financial defaults by cities, local government units and eventually states, as they cannot meet the massive, unfunded obligations, and the federal government has no money to bail them out.
- An increasing flight of productive individuals, individuals with financial resources that are movable and business that can relocate from the disaster states like California and Illinois to the more fiscally-stable

states, and from the failing cities to the suburbs or to safer states. This will, of course, exacerbate the fiscal disaster of those area, but as they go down, they will pull the better-off states with them.

- The Federal Government passes a law to try to prevent individuals and businesses from relocating funds outside the country. It has limited utility, as the wealthy and successful can usually outwit the bureaucrats. States attempt to keep wealth inside their borders by coercion, but have even less success.

- To avoid a similar default, and unable to tax more from a faltering economy, the Federal Government is unable to resist the temptation to pay its debts by printing fiat money. This, in turn produces accelerating inflation, making everyone's savings and income worth far less—a tax on value. Eventually it becomes hyperinflation, such as Zimbabwe[2] and Argentina[3] experienced through similar feckless policies.

- As government at all levels faces fiscal shortfalls, massive numbers of government employees are laid off and entitlements arel not paid. There are "geezer riots." Hoping to generate support for ever higher taxes to kick the can down the road, public officials lay off the popular, visible employees first. Police, firefighters and teachers get the axe ahead of politically-connected administrators of vote-buying programs. Entitlement riots, including violence, spread throughout the country. The recent struggles in Madison, WI become a fond memory of a by-gone, gentler time. Public officials and their families are targeted with arson and violence.

- The cutbacks in police and fire protection in the cities unleash a wave of crime. Both native and imported criminal gangs recruit freely, and parts of the cities become "no go" areas, not just for regular citizens, but for any authority. Governors call out the National Guard to keep order, but are unable to find the funds to sustain them. Gang warfare and murder become as common in the United States as in Mexico.[4] People who are able to do so flee the cities, reducing the tax base and the number of professionals such as doctors, lawyers, accountants and engineers needed to keep the cities' economy viable and infrastructure working. Crime and chaos stalk the urban landscape.

- As Jihadists take over and control Muslim communities, those areas, too, become "no go" areas, as in Europe. Secular Muslims are murdered as apostates and the authorities are unable to intervene for fear of riots, which brings the Muslim population firmly under the control of the Jihadists. Muslim women are forced into the restrictions of *Shari'a* law, and non-Muslim or Westernized Muslim women dare not go in certain areas for fear of gang rape, disfigurement and murder.

- As police protection breaks down in the cities, citizens form vigilante groups to protect themselves from the violent thugs. Street corner "trials" and executions become increasingly common, as do simple retaliatory murders.

- The European Union comes apart as fiscal ruin and bankruptcy[5] overtake countries like Portugal, Ireland, Spain, Greece and Italy and wealthier countries like France, Britain and Germany bolt to try to avoid sinking with them. But demographics rule, and the declining birthrate of native Europeans makes their welfare states, more generous than the US, unsustainable, even in the strongest economies. Entitlement riots spread and open warfare with the underclass in European cities, especially unassimilated, radicalized Muslims accustomed to living on the dole, further destroys European security and the Eurozone economy. The collapse of the Eurozone plunges the world into a depression, multiplying the fiscal and economic problems of the United States. NATO disbands, and the U.S. brings home troops to keep them out of harm's way, because the dollars to sustain them aren't available, and because they are needed at home to enforce martial law in many areas.
- China begins to squeeze us out of the Far East, not with a direct attack, but with economic pressure and threats, using our growing debt as a weapon. They conduct cyber attacks[6] on power grids and industrial control systems to weaken our economy. With declining U.S. support, Taiwan sees the writing on the wall, and makes an accommodation, retaining some limited economic independence and superficial freedoms similar to Hong Kong, as part of the People's Republic. Japan, South Korea and Southeast Asia get the message and drift into China's orbit. India becomes neutral to avoid Chinese support for Pakistan. China's new "Asian Economic Union" takes in these countries as trading partners similar to the European Common Market, and it becomes the world's largest economy.
- Anarchy reigns in cities throughout the developed world, and as they became ungovernable, the military seals them off to protect the still-viable areas on the perimeters. (I predicted this in a science fiction short story I published in 1999.[7])
- The new Hispanic majorities in the southwest begin fighting among themselves, both as the criminal cartels struggled for dominance here as they have in Mexico, and as established Hispanic-American citizens fight to preserve their American way of life from the lawless and less-educated illegal immigrants. Assimilated and better educated American citizens of Hispanic ethnicity who are able to flee to states where they can be safer, worsening the situation of states like California by creating an additional brain and revenue drain.
- All the ills that I suggested would quickly follow a nuclear attack will still take hold, perhaps more slowly. Food production and distribution, the provision of healthcare on a wide basis and the availability of energy and consumer goods all break down. To what extent will not be known until it happens.
- Local warlords arise, ruling areas with iron fists and the support of most

57

people who now put stability, order and safety above democracy and civil rights. These new tribal areas have only a nodding allegiance to Washington or their state capitals, which tolerates them as long as they keep order and produce no further drain on government. the public prefers oppression and food to crime and chaos.

As the country enters this collapse, we don't know where the bottom will be, or how much of the above will come about, or to what extent. We don't know if large portions of the country would still be governable, probably by military rule, or if the nation might fragment into small pieces, controlled by local dictators of various persuasions, abilities and humanity. We don't know if these disasters will lead to yet worse evils. We only know that it would no longer be America as we have loved her and that poverty and oppression would be the order of the day. To get an idea of what a complete collapse of society could look like, I recommend *Wolf and Iron*, a 1990 novel by Gordon R. Dickson.[8]

Yes, this is an apocalyptic vision of the future. But unless you happily cling to the non-reality-based, but comforting "everything works out for the best" philosophy, I don't see how you can read through the source materials about the issues I have addressed and not believe the country faces a desperate situation. If you think these problems can be solved without devastating economic pain, political disruption and a considerable effusion of blood, I hope you are getting the Easter Bunny or Captain America on the job. Soon.

And, doubtless you are asking ...

Chapter Seven: How Did We Get into This Mess?

I will make this chapter short, as by now I have doubtless lost any readers who are transnational progressives, central planning statists, Trotskyite dreamers from academia or garden variety Leftists who believe intentions matter far more than the results of their policies. And I don't want to drive away any more folks before I get to solutions—such as they are—in the following chapter. I believe the quotes below sum up what has happened to the United States and, indeed, to all of western civilization:

"In the end more than they wanted freedom, they wanted security. When the Athenians finally wanted not to give to society but for society to give to them, when the freedom they wished for was freedom from responsibility, then Athens ceased to be free." —Edward Gibbon (Yes, I already used this quote in the *Introduction*. It's worth re-reading and thinking about.)

"Government is the great fiction, through which everybody endeavors to live at the expense of everybody else." -Frederic Bastiat, French Economist (1801-1850)

"Luxury ruins republics; poverty, monarchies." —Charles De Montesquieu

"No snowflake in an avalanche ever feels responsible." —Stanislaw Lem

It started with the Great Depression, when the pressure to do *something* pushed President Hoover to sign the Smoot-Hawley bill destroying international trade. "Before the Great Depression, it was not considered to be the business of the federal government to try to get the economy out of a depression. But the Smoot-Hawley tariff—designed to save American jobs by restricting imports—was one of Hoover's interventions, followed by even bigger interventions by FDR. The rise in unemployment after the stock market crash of 1929 was a blip on the screen compared to the soaring unemployment rates reached later, after a series of government interventions."[1]

Since the 1930s, the growth of government would have staggered earlier presidents, from Jefferson to Cleveland to Coolidge. By the time my Baby Boomer generation came of age, the government had become the first place we turned to solve problems, rather than the last resort. And every time the government "solved" a problem, it created new programs, new government jobs to be paid for by taxes on the private economy, new regulations and paperwork dragging down the private sector and innovation. None of us have clean hands—we all have our favorite "essential programs" that we defend.

Government entitlement programs make up 35% of wages.[2] We maintain the fiction of citizens petitioning their government for the redress of grievances, but the every-growing army of lobbyists in Washington and our state capitals are not there to redress wrongs. The vast majority are there to fight for a larger piece of the government spending pie for the groups they represent. I should know—I've been both a legislator and represented groups that lobby.

When I was a state senator in the 1970s, every year I'd put an "issues" poll in the local newspapers, which voters could clip and send to me. It was totally unscientific, mainly a PR effort, and heavily biased towards my more conservative supporters who tended to respond. I would ask, "What is the worst problem facing Massachusetts?" Of the alternatives listed, "Spending and Taxes" always led by a wide margin. Then I'd ask, "Should the Commonwealth spend more, less or the same in the following areas?" In every area except welfare, large margins said "more" or "the same." They'd say "less" for welfare, but more for "helping children in poverty," pretty much the same thing. Of those who listed taxes and spending as the biggest problem, 70% listed at least one area they wanted more spending in, and 50% listed two or more areas where the government should spend more. I concluded that what the people wanted were lower taxes and higher spending. Politicians of both parties trying to give them that is why we are facing a fiscal collapse.

The massive growth of the modern welfare state has put government beyond the comprehension of most people. They no longer understand it or feel responsible for it as the "owners." Most folks feel they cannot influence government. Those who do seek only to influence that piece that affects them directly, in the pocketbook. The motto we take to our representatives is, "I want more, I will vote for whoever gives me more, and how you pay for more isn't my concern unless it comes from me." They have almost no understanding of economics and few realize that all taxes get passed through to the general public in one way or another.

Let's take just President Johnson's "War on Poverty," one of the massive modern government "problem solving" programs, which has cost $16 trillion over the past 45 years. "Thanks to over $900 billion a year (over 5 percent of GDP) of spending on over 70 means-tested welfare programs spread over 13 government agencies, more than 40 million Americans currently receive food stamps, poverty is higher today than it was in the 1970s, and 40 percent of all children are born outside of marriage."[3]

"In mid-1960s America, the nation's out-of-wedlock birth rate (which stood at 7.7 percent at the time) began a rapid and relentless climb across all demographic lines, a climb that would continue unabated until 1994, when the Welfare Reform Act put the brakes on that trend. Today the overall American illegitimacy rate is about 33 percent (26 percent for whites). For blacks, it hovers at near 70 percent—approximately three times the level of black illegitimacy that existed when the War on Poverty began in 1964."[4] The breakdown of the family, especially the black family by the War on Poverty and the cultural changes of the 1960s has produced an underclass with every incentive to support the growth of government, government spending and politicians who promise them more. " ... two-parent black families are rarely poor."[4]

With 47% of American families paying no federal income taxes[5], and the large number of government workers dependent on increased taxes for their personal income, we have a majority who benefit from ever-more government spending. Add to them the contractors and foundations living off government grants, plus the trial lawyers whose litigation system is government-protected, and you begin to see why even the smallest attempts to cut the Federal budget are pictured as "extremist" attacks on vital programs. The true costs of these programs—even to those who "benefit" from them—are not well understood. Aren't freebies free? Perception is reality.

At the same time that we have had greatly decreased interest and involvement in politics by citizens as owners, sharply increased participation and demands by citizens as members of entitlement groups, and the Sixties-generated collapse of the family and "middle class values," we have had a startling decrease in economic and political literacy. "A groundbreaking multi-year survey of 28,000 students attending 85 U.S. colleges and universities by the Intercollegiate Studies Institute (www.isi.org) found that American institutions of higher learning are not providing students even basic instruction on American history, economics and government—probably not even enough for them to make informed decisions at the ballot box. Even Ivy Leaguers could not pass a multiple-choice test on America's foundational principles"[6] Jay Leno's classic "Jaywalking" series is no longer a funny aberration, but the sad standard for citizens. If college students don't know enough to make intelligent decisions, what hope is there for those with high school educations? What hope for those born into the poverty and desperation of single-parent families who far too often don't finish high school? Or those who are among the 20% of graduates who are functionally illiterate,[7] but pushed through with a sub-standard education to inflate politically-correct graduation rates? What hope for our country?

Yet too many tenure-protected members of the teachers' and professors' unions go on scorning "dead white males," civics education and foundational principles in favor of the political correct nonsense that passes for deep thought in academia today. The result is an electorate where two thirds of Americans can't name *one* of the nine justices on the Supreme Court,[8] making decisions that have great impact on their lives. On the plus side, they know the finalists on *American Idol*.

The upper class elites used to lead America in war; think about John F. Kennedy and George H. W. Bush in WWII. Now the military isn't allowed to even recruit on many campuses. In 1956, "Princeton graduated 400 students who later served in uniform." But by 2004, " ... just nine of the school's graduating class entered the military."[9] Those who benefit the most from our Republic now often give the least back. Military service, like taxes, has become something for the "little people." The result is a military that, as many have noted, is increasingly distant from the civilian society it protects. Thus the bitter bumper sticker, "My kid's in Iraq so your kid can party in college."

The heart despairs. But if death finds us, it must, as was said of John Quincy Adams when he died on the floor of the House of Representatives, find us at the post of duty.

Chapter Eight: What Can You Do to Prevent a Collapse?

Hoo, boy, I knew you were going to ask that. After the case I've laid out, I wish I had some magic fix, some promise of *Hope and Change* if you would only vote for the right person, or take the right, not-too-painful action. There is no easy fix. There never is, the honeyed words of politicians notwithstanding.

Unfortunately, I have only the Churchill solution to offer: Blood, toil, tears and sweat. The more toil, tears and sweat now, the less blood later. But I think bloodshed unavoidable.

The enormity of the challenges is overwhelming. Unfortunately, too many people belong to the "things always happen for a (good) reason" school of wishful thinking, despite the historical record. Too many others think, "There's nothing I can do. So I'll do the best I can for me and my family, and hope things work out."

And a great many people believe there is no problem at all. They think that any concerns expressed about Jihad or illegal immigration are simply the endemic racism of evil America, concern about the deficit is just the rich fighting against paying their "fair share" for "social justice" from the abundant wealth Michael Moore claims America has, and China is a trading partner whose economy is tied to us, so concerns there are probably also rooted in racism or a reflexive McCarthyism and anti-communism. This would include many politicians, most journalists and the vast majority of academics in the "soft sciences."

So we are going to fight this war with a far too many of our fellow citizens absent without leave or, like Jane Fonda during Vietnam, actively aiding the enemies of freedom. And it is a war, the most difficult type of war. This book is a recruiting poster.

If an army of Orcs[1] was pouring over our border, we'd stand shoulder to shoulder, dying in place when necessary. But when the enemy is excessive spending and debt, too many people fight first to protect their own finances, to shift costs and sacrifices to others, and not to protect the society at large. When standing against the "invasion" costs you money, makes your family poorer and earns you epithets like "racist" or "helping the rich," instead of medals and respect, standing for what is right becomes very difficult. As Field Marshal William J. Slim said, "Moral courage is a higher and rarer virtue than physical courage." And moral courage is needed most right now.

Old soldiers have long said, "I will pray like everything depends on God, and fight like everything depends on me." That is not bad advice. The first thing you might pray for is that I'm wrong, or that something will come along to save us.

That, in fact, is one of the reasons we must fight. The longer we can hold the Republic together, with some semblance of the freedoms and opportunities we have enjoyed, the better chance of some game changer, some unanticipated "black swan" development will appear and take the pressure off us.

And we must fight because, if America goes down, there is no place to which we can flee, no country able to offer shelter and the economic and political freedoms America has always offered to immigrants who wanted to be Americans. Churchill said that, "You may come to the moment when you will have to fight with all the odds against you and only a precarious chance of survival. There may even be a worse case. You may have to fight when there is no hope of victory, because it is better to perish than to live as slaves." We are certainly at the "odds against us" moment. If enough of us do not pitch in now, we will soon be at the "no hope of victory" moment.

Strengthen your position

Soldiers and Marines wear body armor and helmets, and dig fighting holes, not because they are afraid, but because they know they need to protect themselves to stay in the fight. The father of Charles Hofmann, my best friend in high school, Ken Hofmann, was a combat infantryman who saw heavy fighting in WWII. When I joined the Marines, he told me he survived the war because he was never too tired to dig in. It's time to dig in to secure positions.

If you are located in one of the fiscal disaster states, or one of the death spiral cities, and your business, your job, your family and/or your financial resources can be relocated to a safer area, do so.

If you can reduce your lifestyle and your debt, putting more resources into things that are inflation proof and useful in a troubled future, do so. I am not advocating that everyone become survivalists or join militias. But if you are comfortable with firearms and knowledgeable about gun safety—or willing to take courses to learn—I think it is wise to arm yourself. If you do, be sure you have an adequate supple of ammunition. As a friend says, "buy it cheap and stack it deep."

The less vulnerable you are to financial changes and social turmoil, the longer you'll be in the fight. I am neither a financial nor a home security expert. But there are people who are and they have written books that will help you. I don't want to create a nation of armed paranoids, but a nation of sheep doesn't seem to be working.

Focus, focus, focus

I believe I've outlined the major challenges to the Republic in this volume. You don't focus on a hangnail when you have cancer. Americans of all stripes spend far too much time fighting over small, hot button issues than over the existential threats.

Ten years from now, it's not going to matter if the cold, hungry lesbian couple living next door are married or not. It will matter a lot if they are armed and willing to help you defend your neighborhood against lawless marauders.

Fifteen years from now it won't matter if Barack Obama was born on Mars. It will matter a great deal if the deficits created during his administration create hyperinflation, destroying the economy and America's ability to deploy a capable military.

And when you can't heat your home, power your lights, feed your family or run your car, Global Warming will not be any higher on your scale of concerns than the great Global Cooling scare of the 1970s.

In short, don't sweat the small stuff.

Educate yourself and then others

Reading this book is a good step, but only a small one. Read the source material, then search for additional material on these topics, including articles that disagree with my points. You can't know too much. Buy copies of this book for your family, your friends and your political representatives. It's cheap, and the royalties go to a good cause, not to me. Read and share the political stories I post on my blog, www.tartanmarine.blogspot.com and the websites I list in the "resources" appendix.

Make sure you are educated in economics, government and history. The point is to be an educated voter, an informed teacher of others, a knowledgeable advocate for freedom and the Republic.

A Reading List for the Educated Voter.

Applied Economics: Thinking Beyond Stage One
by Thomas Sowell

Economics may be called the "dismal science," but a lack of understanding of basic economic principles by most voters and far too many politicians is the root of much of our current trouble. Politicians often get elected by giving voters things they want in the short term, which ruin the economy in the long term, and the voters fail to make the connection. If you don't understand economics, you are not an informed voter.

No one explains economics more clearly than Dr. Sowell, whose economics books are in many languages and many classrooms. His research and examples are strong, and his writing both entertaining and easy to understand for the lay reader. His best-seller *Basic Economics* might be even better, but it's much longer. If you want more, read that as well.

Sowell is well-represented on this list, because I find him both brilliant and excellent at conveying ideas. He was born to a dirt-poor black family in North Carolina that didn't have hot water or electricity, supported himself from age 17, and worked his way (before affirmative action) through Harvard, Columbia and to a PhD from the University of Chicago. He has taught at several major universities and has dozens of books in print. His autobiography, *A Personal Odyssey* is inspiring. His columns are archived on his website: www.tsowell.com.

Race and Culture: A World View
by Thomas Sowell

The challenges of race and culture that confront us are not unique to America. Again, Sowell's excellent research and pertinent examples put these problems into perspective. You will come away with a better understanding and a new view of these issues.

His excellent collection of essays, *Black Rednecks and White Liberals* is also a wonderful book, touching on many of these topics. The "Real History of Slavery" essay is alone worth the price of that book.

A Conflict of Visions: Ideological Origins of Political Struggles
by Thomas Sowell

I might as well get my last recommendation for Sowell out of the way. This book is different from many of his others in that he is not putting forth his ideas, viewpoint and opinions here, but presenting a balanced discussion of the foundations of thought for modern liberalism and modern conservatism. It requires a bit more intellectual focus than the books above, but will not be hated by folks of either viewpoint. If you want to understand why those stupid liberals/conservatives think like they do, this is where to find out.

America Alone: The End of the World As We Know It
by Mark Steyn

Steyn is a very entertaining and amusing writer, though this is a most serious subject. It deals with demographics and the dangerous fact that for most of the Western world, including Japan and Canada, the native birth rate has fallen well below the replacement rate of 2.1 lives births per woman. Unless this can be reversed, which seems unlikely, the cultures of Europe and the West are likely to collapse within 30 years. It also means the Western social welfare state cannot be sustained, and that Europe will increasingly be Islamicized and in fiscal turmoil. America's birthrate is right at 2.1, thanks mostly to Hispanics and some sub-cultures like the Mormons. Since economic progress and liberty has depended on Western civilization, the implications for future generations are scary.

No god but God: The Origins, Evolution, and Future of Islam
by Reza Aslan

This is a pro-Islam view by an Iranian religious scholar. In my view, several of the important questions are glossed over, and being Iranian, he leans a tad toward the Shi'a side of the Sunni-Shi'a struggle, but it's a good, non-inflammatory understanding of how moderate Muslims view their religion. Since the challenge of militant political Islam isn't going away, you had better understand this religion. (BTW, Islam means "submission" not "peace" as is often claimed.)

The Politically Incorrect Guide to Islam (and the Crusades)
by Robert Spencer

This is the other side of the study of Islam, as Spencer is an out-spoken critic of political Islam and the belief that it is basically a "religion of peace." If you read this and *No god but God*, you'll be pretty well grounded in the arguments.

Spencer also wrote *The Complete Infidel's Guide to the Koran, The Truth About Muhammad: Founder of the World's Most Intolerant Religion* and other books that are well researched, and which would get him beheaded in any of a number of countries.

The Sword of the Prophet by Serge Trifkovic and *A Concise History of the Crusades* by Thomas F. Madden are also worth reading. It also helps if you know that Islam attacked Europe well before the much-maligned Crusades and continued those attacks for hundreds of years. See Tours, Battle of, 732 and Constantinople, fall of, 1453.

Sowing the Wind: The Seeds of Conflict in the Middle East
by John Keay

A broad look at an area we will be engaged with for a long time. This is an excellent one-volume history of the Middle East, from 1890 through the Suez crisis in 1956, with an epilog to bring us up to date. The catalog of crime and invasion, contention, execution and insurrection, siege and betrayal, of Hashemite vs. Wahhabi, Sunni vs. Shi'a vs. Kurd vs. Turk, Allies vs. Ottomans, Britain vs. France, Zionists vs. Muslims, and other groups great and small could give a tourist pause, never mind a diplomat or soldier. Critics suggest this is a liberal, blame-the-West view, but I didn't get that impression.

A Peace to End All Peace: Creating the Modern Middle East 1914 – 1922 by David Fromkin is also worth reading, but narrower.

Infidel
by Ayann Hirsa Ali.

What is it like to be a woman under Islam? Ali's autobiography describes her rise from a nomadic Muslim family in Somalia, her and her sister's genital mutilation at ages 5 & 4, her escape to Holland from a forced marriage, her election as a member of the Dutch parliament, her campaign against the domestic violence and circumcision of little girls on kitchen tables—a practice that is widespread among Muslim immigrants in Holland—the murder of Theo van Gogh (grand nephew of the painter) after they made a film together criticizing Muslim violence against women, and her move to the United States after having to go into hiding to save her own life. If there was ever a feminist book by a feminist who sought change at the risk of her life, this is it.

Liberty and Civilization: The Western Heritage
edited by the philosopher Roger Scruton.

The book is described as examining, "the intellectual and spiritual traditions of our belief in individual liberty, from its Judeo-Christian origins on through Enlightenment philosophy." I found several of the essays, such as one on little-known aspects of the history of the women's rights movement, worth the price of the book. (Not that I liked every essay in it.) Valuable to understanding the foundations of our Republic.

Liberty and Tyranny: A Conservative Manifesto
by Mark R. Levin

Levin has a reputation as a ranting bomb-thrower on his radio program. I don't listen to talk radio, so I couldn't say. But this short, concise book is a clear and ringing defense of freedom and individualism. I highly recommend it.

Kicking the Sacred Cow
by James P. Hogan

Hogan is a "hard science" science fiction writer, who got interested in controversies in science and researched them for this book. It's out of print, so a bit hard to get. I'm not a scientist, and I suspect that many, but not all of the alternative theories he explores are wrong. But I was fascinated by the politics, the manipulation, the vicious attacks, and the strenuous efforts to prevent other views from being heard that permeate science, where things apparently get as nasty as any political campaign. You won't think of science and the lofty proclamations of scientists the same way after you have read this book.

The Road to Serfdom
by F. A. Hayek

We are back to economics and philosophy with this classic. I'll let you skip it if you wish, as it is a hard read, that needs a lot of focus, not at all like Sowell. Hayek was writing in Britain in the 1940s, having been driven from his native Austria by the Nazis. He warned the West that tyranny can happen anywhere. Hayek saw little to choose between the National Socialism of Hitler and the International Socialism of Stalin. This is the economic and philosophical case for freedom and for individual versus state economic decision making. For Hayek, the Road to Serfdom is the growth of government.

A Question of Command: Counterinsurgency from the Civil War to Iraq
by Mark Moyar

An excellent history of the type of wars we are likely to be involved in for a long time. A Harvard and Cambridge-trained historian, Dr. Moyar reviews what worked and what didn't, who were good leaders and who failed the test of insurgency warfare. This will help you judge how we are doing in places like Afghanistan, and what the chances of success are. My review of this book was published in *Leatherneck Magazine*.

A Patriot's History of the United States: From Columbus's Great Discovery to the War on Terror
by Larry Schweikart and Michael Patrick Allen.

This is long, but an excellent review of American history, despite a few small errors. It makes no attempt to gloss over things like slavery, but neither does it genuflect to the Political Correctness and anti-Americanism that so many academics wear as a badge of honor. You need to be versed in the history of our

Republic, good and bad, to defend it.

The United States Constitution.

Really. If you haven't read it, or not lately, do so. Let me know if you find the phrase "Separation of Church and State." Also, note that providing for the general welfare is not a power granted to the government. It is the reason the enumerated powers, *and no others*, were granted to the federal government. And I'm told you can download a free copy to your Smartphone.

Reading everything on this list will doubtless take you a couple of weeks, so get on it! Yes, I've read every book listed, but I have a reading advantage—I watch almost no TV.

And educating others is crucial. I don't want you to be shunned by friends and relatives like a multi-level sales pest, but look for opportunities to discuss the issues with those who are open to doing so. Share books and web links with them. Write letters to the editor, or op-ed columns if you have the knack, and call in to talk shows. We need everyone in this fight. Spread the word.

You are not going to sway hard-core Leftists, whose adoration of ever-larger government and statist control of economic planning makes them immutable to facts. If they can defend—or at least overlook—female genital mutilation, honor killings, the stoning of teen rape victims and the hanging of gays as part of the lovely chimera of multiculturalism, you cannot change their minds.

The people who need educating are the mass of uncommitted, uninvolved "independents" who often swing elections, but who can't name their member of Congress. It's a target-rich environment.

Get involved in politics and political campaigns

Every election, some politician portrays it as the most important election in the history of the Republic. In 2012, 2014 and 2016, they will be right.

There will be no candidate who is good on every issue. Indeed, what needs to be done for the Republic to survive is, in my view, so painful that no candidate could advocate for the full program of change needed to win this struggle and hope to get elected.

But there will also be one candidate in every race who is better on these issues than the others. If we insist on purity in our candidates, as the "No RINOs" movement among conservatives does, we will find that even worse people are elected and running things, as happened when the Tea Party gifted the Left with the weakest candidates in the Nevada and Delaware senate races in 2010. So vote, volunteer for campaigns, put up yard signs and bumper stickers (yes, the "liberals" who claim to be for "free speech" will key your car—you should see ours) and contribute funds where you can. Support the best candidates *who have a realistic chance of winning*, in both primaries and general elections.

I tend to support Republicans, on the theory that they are ruining the country at a slower rate. Besides, we don't have enough time left to found and develop a new party.

If you are inclined and able, make your voice heard in protest movements like the Tea Party and against the entitlement riots.

Hall's Rules of Politics

If you are going to get involved, remember the object is to *win on election day*, not to make points or feel satisfied because you slammed the opposition. Here's what you need to remember:

1. Elections are won in the middle. They are usually decided by people who are not too interested in and don't like politics. By voters who are much less informed than activists about current events, government and history—the independents. Think about the people on Leno's popular feature "Jaywalking," all voting.

Think about people being given a ride to the polls on election day who ask the driver, "Who's running?"

On Election Day in 2008, Congress had an approval rating far below that of George Bush—but polls showed that 67% of the voters didn't know that the Democrats controlled that Congress.

It's axiomatic in our system that the Republican has to run to the right to get the presidential nomination, and the Democrat has to run to the left—because that's where the contributors, party activists and many primary voters are. Then to win the election, the two nominees must scramble for the center, lying about what they said to get their party's nomination, because after the nominations, that great middle is finally paying a little attention.

So if you are enjoying feeding red meat to the conservative base, but are turning off folks in the moderate, less-involved middle, you are helping the liberal side win the next election.

2. "It's always an advantage to a public man to be the victim of an outrage." This old saying was frequently quoted by my floor leader, the late Senator John Parker, and he had several examples in his political humor books *If Elected, I Promise* and *The Fun and Laughter of Politics*. I recommend them if you can find them.

In 1972, during a poorly watched debate on a small cable TV station, my opponent, the Democrat incumbent, lost his cool, refused to shake hands, yelled at me and called me a "snide, slimy young man." Oh, joy. My research into his temper, campaign style and my efforts to make him angry paid off. Thanks for the "outrage," Joe. I won by nine votes. Doubtless because of this one incident, which we were able to play up, I served five terms as a state senator. His political career ended.

If you are giving the opposition the opportunity to play the victim card, even if it's unreasonable in your view, you are giving them an advantage over you.

3. Perception is reality. This goes with the above. Your intent doesn't matter. What matters is how your actions and deeds are perceived by others, particularly by those in the middle who will decide the outcome of the election. And that perception will be created for a lot of people by the mainstream media,

70

which has taken on the role of Joseph Gobbles for the Left. You can't control how they spin things, but you can be careful not to gratuitously give them anything to spin, anything that feeds their narrative.

Their narrative is that you and other people who care about the issues in this book are greedy, heartless, racist, rich, uncaring, ignorant Yahoos, religious fanatics, uneducated, elite, corrupt, dangerous, violent, and fanatics. That some of these may be mutually exclusive is irrelevant.

4. The Norm Thompson Rule. Norm, a wise selectman in Lunenburg, MA, asked me at an election night party if I wanted to know his theory of politics. Since he'd been elected to office several times, and I was a college student just starting my first campaign, I said sure.

"I want a fellow to be for me," Norm said. "If he won't be for me, I want him neutral. But if he has to be against me, I don't want him mad at me—he'll work twice as hard and give twice as much money if he's mad!"

I carved it in stone on my heart. Sure, the big-government statists are going to hate you. It's the average guy you don't want to make mad, because you don't want him contributing to and campaigning for the opposition.

Our position must be principled and firm, but friendly and inclusive. Reasonable and willing to reason, but not willing to compromise our freedoms away. As Ayn Rand said, "In any compromise between good and evil, it is only evil that can profit."[4]

Actions to avoid

Richard Nixon famously said that he gave his enemies a sword, and they used it to destroy him. Every day, some opponents of Obama and the Left give them, at the least, a club. Here's how to avoid helping the opposition:

1. Avoid the appearance of racism. It was inevitable that, when Obama's policies ran into trouble, the Left and the sycophant mainstream media would play the race card. It happens whenever a black politician gets into policy or ethical trouble.

Yes, there were people who voted for McCain because he was white, and Obama wasn't. Yes, there were a lot of people, blacks and white liberals out to feel warm and fuzzy, who voted for Obama because he was black and McCain wasn't. The percentage of blacks voting for Obama in the primaries was a lot larger than the percentage of whites voting for Hillary. And Obama got more white votes than Kerry or Gore did. All that doesn't matter. People for whom race is a determining factor are going to vote for or against Obama as their biases direct. Our targets are those undecided folks in the middle who are not into identity politics, but who will feel sympathy for Obama if the Left or the mainstream media can use anything—I mean anything—that portrays the opposition to him as being based on race.

Don't tell jokes or circulate items that could be construed as racist. No mention of Africa, color or anything that might be taken as a racial stereotype. No pictures of Obama as a monkey (yes, the Left did that to Bush, but Bush couldn't play the race card.) I'm sure the doctor who was pilloried for forwarding the cartoon of Obama as a witchdoctor was thinking of bad medicine, not race. But it allowed the opposition to discredit him. Don't feed the trolls.

As people who believe in American values, we oppose candidates because of their policies, their actions, or their character, not their race, gender, ethnicity or religion. Or, unlike the Left, their age.

2. Violence and guns. Some idiot wrote a column suggesting a military coup against Obama might be needed. Another created a poll asking if Obama should be killed. And stupid websites put them up. What a gift to the Left's efforts to portray opponents of their statist policies as violent nuts.

The black guy who took a military-appearing rifle (an "assault rifle" to the mainstream media) to the protest outside Obama's Arizona speech was, I asume, an opponent of Obama. But he gave a gift to the mainstream media, as MSNBC was able to film him from the waist down, so viewers couldn't see he was black, and then comment on how people hate Obama because of his race. Do not take guns or weapons to protests. If you take a butter knife, the mainstream media will jump on it to portray you as the equivalent of a Nazi SS Panzer division, marching on Washington. No jokes about guns or violence. It feeds the narrative they are selling to the decent folks in the middle, who are not paying a lot of attention.

3. Don't overplay your hand. The first rule of poker is that you bluff on a weak hand, you underplay a strong hand. The classic political case of overplaying a strong hand was the stupid—no other word for it—Republican attempt to impeach Bill Clinton. They could have left him weakened and twisting in the wind. Instead they gave him and the Democrats the chance to say it was about politics and about sex when it was about perjury—apparently the Democrats believed that if you are charged with sexual harassment, lying under oath is fine.

The whole mess allowed Clinton to portray himself as a victim of Republican politics, and make a remarkable recovery. Suppose Republicans had said, "We believe that perjury is a serious crime, an impeachable offence. We also believe that allowing it to go unpunished in a sexual harassment case jeopardizes the rights of women in future cases. But we know that removing a president from office is also very serious, and we don't believe it should be a partisan endeavor. Therefore, unless and until a significant number of Democrats believe that perjury in sexual harassment cases is an impeachable offence, we do not think that moving forward is in the interests of the country." That would have left him hanging around Democrat necks, defending perjury as opposed to a woman's right to a fair trial in a harassment case.

And suppose they had removed Clinton. President Al Gore would have gone into the 2000 election leading a fired-up Democrat party. Great result for Republicans, right?

You can make more points with the independents by calmly presenting the facts and letting people make up their own minds. Let them discover how bad leftist policies are for America. (Give them a copy of this book!)

4. Focus on the important. You don't have to beat up the opposition for every little thing they do, and doing so makes our cause look petty and desperate. This is often a case of feeding the base, while turning off the votes in the middle you need to win.

5. Don't overreach. This goes with not overplaying your hand. Nothing is more common in politics than to overreach by taking a strong case and hard facts, and then moving into speculation, and sometimes into lies. And then your whole case comes crashing down.

I contributed to the Swift Boat Vets, but I think they overreached. They had a strong case, based on facts. Kerry did launch his career by denigrating his fellow veterans in the Winter Soldier Project, which was largely based on lies. Then they got into speculation about his medals, something they couldn't prove. That gave the opposition ammo to question their entire case and create the impression they were unfair—aided by the mainstream media. Maybe Kerry deserved his medals—I wasn't there. If not, frankly he wouldn't be the only officer in Vietnam to get a medal on the cheap.

I don't know if Obama was born in Hawaii or not. Some people will never be convinced, regardless of the evidence either way. But, I've stayed away from the Birther movement, because I can see them overreaching, thus aiding Obama. To me, it was clear that no court would overturn the results of an election, even if you had a video of him being born on Mars. And especially not when it would likely result in riots, destruction and murder in the inner cities. Too much of the Birther movement has used speculation or documents that aren't credible, thus tainting all associated with it. I'm focused on policy.

6. Avoid personal attacks. Congressman Joe Wilson fired up the base and he took in a lot of campaign dollars. But he allowed the mainstream media and Obama to shift the focus off the lies in Obama's speech to Joe Wilson's "You Lie" outburst. It was a gift to Obama. See the note about being the victim of an outrage.

If Wilson had issued a press release the next day saying that the President's statements were untrue because of X, Y and Z, there would have been no more outrage than there was at Obama calling his opponents liars in that same speech.

Calling the President a liar is a personal attack. Saying that, "Yesterday, President Obama spoke about a man who died from cancer because he couldn't get insurance, but in fact, that man did get coverage and lived for four more years," lets voters conclude that the President is a liar, without you making him a victim by saying so.

Attack policies. Attack actions. Exposing actions and bad policies will expose the character flaws and lack of judgment without resorting to personal attacks that may give your opponent the sympathy of swing voters.

7. Avoid the direct insult. Saying, "President Obama is a liar" is a direct insult. Saying, "President Obama has such a great reverence for the truth that he doesn't want to wear it out by overuse" is satire, clever and more likely to score points with the swing voters. Humor and ridicule are powerful weapons—

if directed at his policies and actions, and not at him personally.

Ridicule is an effective weapon. But, again, we want to ridicule the policies and the actions, not the individual personally. Never mind how the Left treated Bush, Palin, *et al.* The infantry have a saying: "Take the high ground, or they will bury you in the valley!" I've found it to be true in politics as well. It's hard to stay calmly on the high ground, of course, especially if you are angry, but it's generally the safest and best policy. Coming down off the high ground makes you vulnerable to counter attack.

8. Act with integrity. Some of the phony documents circulated in the Birther movement have helped Obama the same way Dan Rather's phony military documents helped Bush. Don't forward Internet glurge without at least trying to check it out. Don't forward things you know to be untrue. Hitting "send" without checking is a gift to the statists. If we are the good guys, we have to try to act with integrity. Leave the lies and phony documents to the Left and their mainstream media allies.

Have I ever violated any of the above? Of course. I'm hardly perfect, and in fact I believe perfection doesn't exist. But constant improvement does, and we can all improve how well we act, every day. And the better we can do following these rules, the less we feed the statist trolls who are destroying America.

Here's one more good maxim I don't always follow: "Anger is a good servant, but a bad master." It's especially true in politics.

What are you working for?

You need to fight for policies that will drastically cut government spending at all levels. What needs to be done is very painful. It will put you in the line of fire from government unions, which will include death threats (as in Wisconsin) and perhaps violence from the thugs. This will be harder than a shooting war, because many of your fellow citizens will be scrambling to grab a bigger share of a shrinking pie, rather than standing with you.

Whole departments and programs of the federal government need to be eliminated. Think of the cries of outrage to eliminating the Departments of Energy and Education, or of farm subsidies. Think of the fights over entitlements. Even the less painful suggestions for fixing Social Security draw overwhelming opposition. Charles Krauthammer, for example, suggested we should, "Raise the retirement age, tweak the indexing formula (from wage inflation to price inflation) and means-test so that Warren Buffett's check gets redirected to a senior in need."[2] That's a start, but the fight will be hard, and fixing Medicare will be worse. You will often be fighting for policies that are not in your short-term financial self-interest.

You need to fight for policies that will secure the border and restrict illegal immigration, while welcoming those legal immigrants who wish to be productive American citizens, to speak English and to be assimilated into our culture of freedom and success. If you oppose one illegal criminal entering the U.S., politicians wanting to cater to the Hispanic vote and leftists who reflexively oppose anything that will preserve American culture will try to tar you with the racist brush. You will have to bear up under this abuse.

You need to fight the Left's racist immigration policies, where groups like, for example, the Hmong have to work hard and jump through many hoops to become citizens, but others often get a pass to stay as illegals, because of politics. This hurts Americans of Hispanic ancestry as much as anyone.

You must fight to oppose both the violent and the stealth Jihads. You must work to prevent the imposition of *Shari'a* law on us, and on secular Muslims who came to America to escape its tyranny. You must support them when they have the courage to speak out against the *Shari'a* abuse of women. You must honor them when they work to reform Islam, as the other great faiths have been reformed, to be compatible with modern civilization and political liberty.

And, perhaps conflicting with the need for fiscal restraint, you must fight to keep America's military strong enough to both fight the asymmetrical insurgency posed by the violent Jihad and to counter the growth of conventional military power of a China seeking to dominate its neighbors, many of whom are vital allies and trading partners of the US.

Needed political reforms (a secondary target)

We also need political reform that would help us—the owners of this Republic—better direct the fortunes of our Republic. I believe the following changes are needed, but have little chance of being enacted.

Presidential Primaries should use the Graduated Random Presidential Primary System,[3] which is designed to begin with contests in small-population states, where candidates do not need tens of millions of dollars in order to compete.

Convention Delegates should be elected by Congressional District, rather than winner take all in each state. This gives unknown candidates or local favorites a chance to garner delegates and get national attention. Delegates should be required to be residents of the congressional district they are elected from. Delegates would be legally bound to the candidate on the first vote at the party's convention.

Third Parties receiving 5% of the national popular vote in the last presidential election should automatically be included on the ballot in the Primary System, unless they failed to run delegates in 75% of the Congressional Districts. Other parties wishing to run in the November election would need to file signatures in each state equal to1% of the votes cast in that state in the last election.

These numbers are suggestions—I was not handed a tablet with them on top of a mountain.

The **Electoral College** should be retained, but reformed to do away with electors. A state's electoral vote sould be certified by its Secretary of State or chief elections officer just like any other vote. This eliminates the specter of a rogue or corrupt elector changing the outcome.

Secondly, we should award two electoral votes to the candidate who won the state, and the others to the winner of each Congressional District, as Maine and Nebraska do now. This would put every state in play and mean that the parties couldn't write off any state. Republicans could win votes in California, Democrats in Texas. Campaigns would be much more national.

All election voting should be done by computers, and every election should require a candidate to receive 50% plus 1 of the vote in order to win. You would vote with a number one for your first choice, two for your second choice and so on. If no candidate is the first choice of 50% of the voters, the candidate with the lowest number of first place votes is eliminated, and those votes are automatically apportioned to the other candidates based on who received the number two vote. And so on, until one candidate has a majority. While assuring majority rule, this would give third parties and independents a chance to be elected or at least influence the outcome, and let voters vote their first choice without helping the worst candidate.

Congressional Districts should be set by an independent commission, using a computer model which does not take party registration or voting history into account.

Term Limits are needed. We should limit Presidents to one six-year term. Then the President can spend six years fighting for things he or she believes are right for the country, without an eye on re-election, and would not need to spend tax dollars buying votes for the next campaign. We need term limits for members of Congress. The power they have to raise funds and the creation of a permanent political class is not good for the country. I'd favor changing both senators and house members to having four-year terms, half elected every two years, with a limit of four terms in each body. I understand and have agreed with the philosophical arguments against term limits, but the government has become so large and remote and the power of incumbents to buy votes with borrowed money so huge, I now think they are needed. I'd also increase the restriction on lobbying by both former members and by former staff members to four years, making them spend a term outside Washington.

Line item veto power must be given to the President on budgets. No more should he or she be able to avoid responsibility for earmarks, pork projects and excessive spending by claiming a need to sign the budget as a whole, even with terrible things in it.

A list of all **earmarks** for individual House and Senate members should be circulated to every member, and each member would be required to sign off supporting or opposing each earmark. That signoff list should be public record. An earmark that doesn't get 50% approval in the process could not be included in the budget except by a roll call vote in both branches.

Bills should be **published on the Internet**, with full public access, a minimum of three days before they are voted on or amendments offered. Once the amendment process is completed, they should be on the Internet a minimum of three days before final passage. No more "vapor bills."

Congress should not be allowed to **exempt itself** or congressional staff from laws it passes that apply to the country or citizens at large.

We should prohibit bills that have not had public hearings from being substituted for other bills to avoid the regular process.

All tax cuts must be permanent; all tax increases must sunset, and may be renewed only by a roll call vote and two-thirds majority.

We should require that proposed **amendments must be germane** to the legislation. That is, legislators should not be able to attach an amendment on abortion or guns to a bill on National Parks, avoiding the committee process. Nor should they be able to use a bill as a "shell," wiping out everything in it and substituting a completely different bill that has not gone through the legislative process with hearings.

Let's have real transparency. No excluding the press, the public or members of the other party from meetings between legislators or legislators and executive branch officials about the contents or details of legislation.

It should be illegal for **government employees to unionize**. All such unions are conspiracies between politicians and public employees against the taxpayers and fiscal stability. In the end, they will destroy themselves by destroying the government, the way a morbidly obese person destroys himself by eating.

The number of **employees of the Federal Government** should be reduced by 2% per year until the total is reduced by 20%. Only combat troops would be exempt as long as we are at war.

Federal spending should be limited to 20% of GDP by Constitutional amendment, being reduced 1% a year until we hit that target.

We need comprehensive tort reform, including caps on non-economic damages, which will bring down the cost of healthcare, bringing drugs to market, and almost everything else. We lead the world on the percentage of GDP spent on litigation[5]—this is not sustainable.

We need a system where in **civil actions the loser pays**, to reduce frivolous litigation. Curiously, this is one feature of European culture the Obama administration has *not* embraced.

Trail lawyers should be paid at an hourly rate, as is the case in many countries. Taking a percentage of the award, which leads to lottery lawsuits, should be outlawed, or at least strongly discouraged. Yes, this might interfere with the Constitutional right to contract. How about requiring disclosure of the fee arrangements to the jury, so they understand just who is being "made whole" by their decision?

It should be made much easier for attorneys who bring cases **ruled to be frivolous** to have their licenses suspended.

In criminal cases, **expert witnesses** should be selected by the court from lists developed in advance for impartiality, not by the opposing parties. Currently the testimony tends to favor the side paying the bills, leading to dueling witnesses and confusion for the jury. Of course, defendants may have a Constitutional right to call their own experts, but the jury should know if they are paid for their testimony.

Lawyers should be **licensed by the state** in a vetting process that excludes their union, the Bar Association.

You can't do it all. None of us can fix everything. and I may be wrong about some of these reforms.

You can't work on every issue that needs change—real change, not slogans. And the political changes I recommend above are certainly secondary to the immediate need to address the debt, immigration, Jihad and China. But you must do what you can, as much as you can, where and when you can. We all must.

And you must do it all again next week. And the week after. And probably throughout your whole life, because if we are to preserve the American Republic, it will be a long, slow, painful, uphill slog.

Unless there is a very rapid collapse of America, my age and health situation means I will not see the outcome of this struggle. Many of us will not. But if we fail, our great-grandchildren will curse our memories.

Conclusion

The most obvious criticism "disaster deniers" will level at this book is that I cherry-picked articles and facts to support my conclusions.

That is not accurate. I came to the conclusions *because* of reading innumerable articles on these subjects, both before I started my blog, and as the blog grew, with its flood of daily information. Since I've finished the first draft, even more damning information has come to my in-box. *Standard and Poor*, for example, "changed its outlook on the United States from 'stable' to 'negative' and said the federal government could lose its AAA rating if officials fail to bring spending in line with revenue."[1] There will be many more news stories and articles, the vast majority negative, before I can get this in your hands, but at some point I had to stop writing and publish.

Finding supporting facts and opinions wasn't difficult. You will note that most of my references were from material published early in 2011, as I was writing this. Winnowing through the deluge of supporting material that fills my daily in-box was the challenge. If I thought of a topic on which I hadn't saved an article, an Internet search always gave me hundreds or thousands of hits on it. Few of them contradicted my fears. There were, in fact, far too many articles on these issues, and deciding when to stop including references or writing on a topic was difficult

Suppose I'm wrong?

Fine. Let us assume I'm wrong, and that you are confident that the Republic will survive and perhaps thrive. Are these still not major problems that will make life difficult for us and our fellow citizens? Will not working to solve them improve America? Will "kicking the can down the road," that is, postponing them for our children to face be the responsible thing to do? You don't have to believe the country is going to collapse to pitch in and work to overcome the challenges these problems present us.

If you don't think there is likely to be a collapse, I fervently hope you are right and I'm wrong. And, given that I'm about past the average survival time for my disease, pulmonary fibrosis, I hope I live long enough for you to say, "I told you so!"

I tend to have an optimistic, upbeat, fairly sunny personality. Or so I think. So why am I so pessimistic? Because the "perfect storm" these four factors create makes it vastly harder to deal successfully with any one of them.

One of my oldest friends is Ron "Count" Pittenger, a fellow Marine I met at Camp Geiger in December of 1964, while we were awaiting shipment to Marine Electronics School in San Diego. Ron recently wrote a comment on my blog about dealing with problems, which I saved for this book: "Over the course of a lifetime, I've noticed that while a single major problem might kill you, usually it can be overcome. The difficulty is that when there are multiple problems at the same time, solving them becomes much more difficult. Two simultaneous problems are four times as difficult to solve as either one alone, three problems at once, nine times as difficult."

Exactly. So, four major disasters threatening our country, culture and way of life will be sixteen times as difficult to overcome.

Hope is not lost, but time is short, the situation desperate and the issue is in doubt. We need you in the frontline.

In 1983, Jerry Pournelle wrote in *There Will Be War*, "To stand on the firing parapet and expose yourself to danger; to stand and fight a thousand miles from home when you're all alone and outnumbered and probably beaten; to spit on your hands and lower the pike; to stand fast over the body of Leonidas the King; to be rear guard at Kunu-Ri; to stand and be still to the Birkenhead Drill; these are not rational acts. They are often merely necessary."

You are now a soldier in a very different kind of war.

To fight for government spending cuts that will hurt your personal finances, perhaps gravely; to take public positions that will get you excoriated as racist or Islamophobic in order to silence you; to risk personal relationships with family and friends to fight for what is needed; to work to educate the uninvolved who would rather stay in their little bubble of denial; to invest dollars and time and effort into political campaigns for candidates who are not all that great on these issues—just better than their opponents; to put yourself at financial and perhaps personal risk fighting for policies and political reforms with scant hope of success; these are not rational acts.

They are merely necessary if we are to give our Republic a chance to survive.

Appendix: Resources for more information

The sites below will provide you with updated information on the issues covered in this book.

US Debt Clock
http://www.usdebtclock.org/
Lots of depressing detail.

National Debt by Year
http://www.treasurydirect.gov/govt/reports/pd/histdebt/histdebt_histo5.htm
For additional reference on the debt

Eat the Rich video
http://www.realclearpolitics.com/video/2011/03/31/bill_whittle_on_eating_the_rich.html
This really puts the deficit in perspective.

Brother, Can You Spare A Trillion?: Government Gone Wild!
http://www.youtube.com/watch?v=VtVbUmcQSuk
Another site putting the debt in understandable terms.

National Center for Policy Analysis
www.ncpa.org
This is a free-market think tank. They have a daily free e-newsletter you can subscribe to that summarizes five or six articles about fiscal policy, healthcare, the environment and other current issue. A good way to get the meat of these issues in a bite-size format.

Thomas Sowell's Webpage
www.tsowell.com
With archive links to his columns and lists of his books. In my view, Dr. Sowell is the most cogent and articulate thinker on economics, politics, culture and race in America today. Of course, he had the benefit of Marine Corps training, back in the 1950s. If you read his books—any of his books—and columns, you can't help becoming smarter and more knowledgeable about these issues.

The Heritage Foundation
http://www.heritage.org
Good source of research and articles on free markets and limited government. If you join, however, expect to get a lot financial solicitations.

The American Thinker
http://americanthinker.com/
Excellent source of articles and columns on these topics

The Patriot Post
http://patriotpost.us/
Free e-newsletters of topics and columns of interest. Also on-point political humor.

The Daily Caller
http://dailycaller.com/
Excellent source of opinion and news.

Real Clear Politics
http://dailycaller.com/
Excellent source of opinion, news and polling.

The Cato Institute
http://www.cato.org/
From their site: A "public policy research organization — a think tank — dedicated to the principles of individual liberty, limited government, free markets and peace. Its scholars and analysts conduct independent, nonpartisan research on a wide range of policy issues."

Red State
http://redstate.com/
Blog including a free e-newsletter of conservative political information and comment.

Judicial Watch
http://www.judicialwatch.org/
Another good source of news on these topics

American Enterprise Institute for Public Policy Research
http://www.aei.org/
A think tank that their website says: "sponsors original research on the world economy, U.S. foreign policy and international security, and domestic political and social issues. AEI is dedicated to preserving and strengthening the foundations of a free society—limited government, competitive private enterprise, vital cultural and political institutions, and vigilant defense—through rigorous inquiry, debate, and writing."

Americans for Immigration Reform
http://www.americansforimmigrationreform.com/
Good source for immigration information.

Immigration Gumballs
https://mail.google.com/mail/?hl=en&shva=1#inbox
Good visual of what immigration means.

The Dark Side of Illegal Immigration
http://www.usillegalaliens.com/
A well documented collection of the problems of illegal immigration

Jihad Watch
www.jihadwatch.com
This site tracks stories worldwide on the Jihad and actions of Islamist extremists. They have a daily free e-newsletter you can subscribe to, which will link you to interesting, if depressing, news stories. Robert Spencer, who maintains the site, has written several books critical of radical Islam. I would not want to accompany him on a speaking tour of Muslim countries.

Muslims in America
http://www.youtube.com/watch?v=OLK1Xpc7SMQ
Video of the collapsing demographics in the developed world

Maps of War
http://www.mapsofwar.com/images/EMPIRE17.swf
Good visual of how Muslim conquests have changed the world map

The Religion of Peace
http://www.thereligionofpeace.com/
Another source for articles on Jihad

Gates of Vienna
http://gatesofvienna.blogspot.com/
Another source for articles on Jihad

Islamic Statements Against Terrorism
http://www.unc.edu/~kurzman/terror.htm
There are moderate Muslims who speak out, however much their voices are drowned in gunfire and explosions.

Investigative Project on Terrorism
http://www.investigativeproject.org/
Good source of information on the threat we face.

The Iconoclast - New English Review
http://www.newenglishreview.org/The_Iconoclast/
Good source for commentary on Jihad issues

"Islamic law" on *WikiIslam* (A critical view)
http://wikiislam.net/wiki/Islamic_law

"Sharia" on Wikipedia (A more benign view)
http://en.wikipedia.org/wiki/Sharia

"Islamic Law: Myths and Realities"
http://www.witness-pioneer.org/vil/Articles/shariah/ilw_myth_real.html
Office of International Criminal Justice at the University of Illinois. This is a pro-Islam site, but note it says, "The most difficult part of Islamic Law for most westerners to grasp is that there is no separation of church and state. The religion of Islam and the government are one."

"Islam 101" on Jihad Watch
http://www.jihadwatch.org/islam-101.html
A critical examination

Islamist Watch
http://www.islamist-watch.org/
From their site: Islamist Watch, a project of the Middle East Forum, combats the ideas and institutions of lawful Islamism in the United States and throughout the West. Arguing that "radical Islam is the problem, moderate Islam is the solution," we seek to expose the Islamist organizations that currently dominate the debate, while identifying and promoting the work of moderate Muslims. Islamist Watch specifically does not deal with counterterrorism but works to establish that lawful Islamism is by and of itself a threat.

Muslims for Progressive Values
http://www.mpvusa.org/
Their values are worth reading, and could get them killed in any number of places.

Chapter References

Where possible, I have included the URL for these sources, so readers can find and pursue the full article on the web. However, given the Internet, some of these URLs may not work by the time your read this. A Google search for the title will usually turn up the full article, and a search on the topics in this book will turn up more information than you can read in a lifetime.

I am not a trained researcher. Since I have tried to draw from a variety of viewpoints, you may question the credibility of some of these sources. I recommend that you read as many of the source articles as possible, both to judge their credibility and to get the extensive details I was not able to include. And I recommend you research these topics through Internet searches, and read other sources and commentary I was not able to include. While you will find evidence countering each on my concerns, I think the total body of evidence will strongly support my contention that these four areas constitute major threats to America and to Western civilization, and that taken together, they are very likely to overwhelm us.

Introduction: Will There Be a Collapse?

1. Davies, Stephen, "The Great Horse Manure Crisis of 1894." *The Freeman*, 9/2004. This excellent article points out the danger of doomsday predictions. http://www.thefreemanonline.org/columns/our-economic-past-the-great-horse-manure-crisis-of-1894/

2. Sowell, Thomas, "A Mind-Changing Page." *Townhall.com*, 6/7/2010. http://townhall.com/columnists/ThomasSowell/2010/06/17/a_mind-changing_page

Chapter One: The Federal Government is Broke. Really

1. Attali, Jacques, "The West and the Tyranny of Public Debt," *Newsweek*, December 27, 2010
http://www.newsweek.com/2010/12/27/the-west-and-the-tyranny-of-public-debt.html
This article is a "Must read."

2. Miron, Jeffery, "The Negative Consequences of Government Expenditure," *The Mercatus Center* at George Washington University, November, 2010. http://mercatus.org/sites/default/files/publication/Negative%20 Consequences%20Government%20Expenditure.MoP_.Miron_.11.9.10.pdf

3. Milbank, Dana, "From Greece, an economic cautionary tale for the U.S.," *Washington Post*, March 9, 2010.
http://www.washingtonpost.com/wp-dyn/content/article/2010/03/08/AR2010030803491.html

4. Thornton, Donal, "Ireland has the highest national debt in Europe," *Irish Central*, April 23, 2010.
http://www.irishcentral.com/business/Ireland-has-highest-national-debt-in-Europe-91899264.html

5. Smith, Donna, "U.S debt to rise to $19.6 trillion by 2015," *Reuters*, June 8, 2010.
http://www.reuters.com/article/idUSN08846252010o608

6. Norton, Leslie P., "China's Sure bet," *Barron's*, November 8, 2010
http://online.barrons.com/article/SB50001424052970203281504575590290564950892.html#articleTabs_panel_article%3D1

7. Fry, Eric, "Why Bernanke's 'Quantitative Easing' Isn't Fooling Anyone," *The Daily Reckoning*, 11/15/10.
http://dailyreckoning.com/why-bernankes-quantitative-easing-isnt-fooling-anyone/

8. Swanson, Gerald J., "Hyperinflation: Lessons from South America." *The Freeman*, January, 1988.
http://www.thefreemanonline.org/columns/hyperinflation-lessons-from-south-america/

9. Villarreal, Pamela, "Social Security and Medicare Projections: 2009." *National Center for Policy Analysis*, June 11, 2009.
http://www.ncpa.org/pub/ba662

10. Smith, Charles Hugh, "Social Security Is in Far Worse Shape Than You Think," *Daily Finance*, January 19, 2011.
http://www.dailyfinance.com/story/retirement/social-security-far-worse-shape-than-you-think/19804267/?icid=maing%7Cmain5%7Cdl2%7Csec1_lnk5%7C37184

11. Ohlemacher, Stephen, "Social Security posting $600B deficit over 10 years" *Associated Press* January 27, 2011.
http://news.yahoo.com/s/ap/20110127/ap_on_re_us/us_social_security

12. Hawkins, John, "4 Reasons The American Dream Will Be Over Unless We Act," *Town Hall*, November 10, 2009.
http://townhall.com/columnists/JohnHawkins/2009/11/10/4_reasons_the_american_dream_will_be_over_unless_we_act

13. Ohlemacher, Stephen, "Nearly half of US households escape fed income tax," *Associated Press*, April 7, 2010.
http://finance.yahoo.com/news/Nearly-half-of-US-households-apf-1105567323.html?x=0

14. Frates, Chris, "Medicare 'doc fix' may cost $200B" *Politico*, February 2, 2010.
http://www.politico.com/news/stories/0210/32335.html

15. Wolf, Richard, "Doctors limit new Medicare patients" *USA Today*, June 21, 2010.
http://www.usatoday.com/news/washington/2010-06-20-medicare_N.htm

16. "Military Retirement: Key Elements and Issues" *CRS Issues Brief for Congress*, March 14, 2006.
http://www.fas.org/sgp/crs/natsec/IB85159.pdf

17. Bumiller, Elizabeth and Shanker, Thom, "Gates Seeking to Contain Military Health Costs" *New York Times*, November 28, 2010
http://www.nytimes.com/2010/11/29/us/29tricare.html

18. "VA 2011 Budget Fast Facts"
http://www.va.gov/budget/docs/summary/Fy2011_Fast_Facts_VA_Budget_Highlights.pdf

19. Isaacs, Katelin P. "Federal Employees' Retirement System: Budget and Trust Fund Issues" *Penny Hill Press*, January 13, 2011.
http://economic-legislation.blogspot.com/2011/01/federal-employees-retirement-system.html

20. Sowell, Thomas, "Is Barney Frank" *Townhall.com* October 21, 2010. http://townhall.com/columnists/ThomasSowell/2010/10/21/is_barney_frank

21. Waters, Maxine, "We do not have a crisis at Freddie Mac and particularly Fannie Mae under the outstanding leadership of Frank Raines" http://blog.beliefnet.com/reformedchicksblabbing/2008/09/maxine-waters-we-do-not-have-a.html

22. "Taxpayers get costly legal bills for Fannie Mae and Freddie Mac" *New York Times*, January 25, 2011.
http://www.tampabay.com/news/business/banking/taxpayers-get-costly-legal-bills-for-fannie-mae-and-freddie-mac/1147427

23. Appelbaum, Binyamin, "Cost of Seizing Fannie and Freddie Surges for Taxpayers" *New York Times*. June 19, 2010.
http://www.nytimes.com/2010/06/20/business/20foreclose.html

24. Riedl, Brian, "New CBO Budget Baseline Reveals Permanent Trillion-Dollar Deficits" *Heritage Foundation*, January 26, 2011.
http://www.heritage.org/Research/Reports/2011/01/New-CBO-Budget-Baseline-Reveals-Permanent-Trillion-Dollar-Deficits

25. Moore, Stephen and Vedder, Richard, "Higher Taxes Won't Reduce the Deficit" *Wall Street Journal*, November 21, 2010.
http://online.wsj.com/article/SB10001424052748704648604575620502560925156.html

26. U.S. Debt Clock
http://www.usdebtclock.org/

Chapter Two: The States are Broke too. So are the Cities.

1. "States hide trillions in debt," *WatchDog.org*, July 23, 2010.
http://watchdog.org/5939/states-hide-trillions-in-debt/

2. Weisenthal, Joseph, "Wow: Texas Deficit Estimate Comes In Worse Than The Worst Expectations" *Business Insider*, January 10, 2011.
http://www.businessinsider.com/texas-budget-shortfall-2011-1

3. Adams, Steven Allen, "State and Local Government Spending Outpaces Private Sector," *Watchdog.com*. August 18, 2010.
http://watchdog.org/6238/state-and-local-government-spending-outpaces-private-sector/

4. Sowell, Thomas, "Benefits of low tax rates in plain sight for all to see," *San Angelo Standard Times*, December 2, 2010.
http://www.gosanangelo.com/news/2010/dec/02/benefits-of-low-tax-rates-in-plain-sight-for-all/

5. Goldmacher, Shane, "Estimated state budget deficit reaches $25.4 billion," *Los Angles Times*, November 11, 2010.
http://articles.latimes.com/2010/nov/11/local/la-me-state-budget-20101111

6. Jones, Tim, "Illinois Has Days to Plug $13 Billion Deficit That Took Years to Produce" *Bloomberg*, January 3, 2011.
http://www.bloomberg.com/news/2011-01-03/illinois-must-plug-13-billion-deficit-in-days-that-took-years-to-produce.html

7. McNichol, Elizabeth, Oliff, Phil and Johnson, Nicholas, "States Continue to Feel Recession's Impact" *Center on Budget and Policy Priorities*, January 21, 2011
http://www.cbpp.org/cms/index.cfm?fa=view&id=711

8. "Moody's Says Pension Holes May Hurt US State Ratings" *aiCIO*, January 28, 2011.
http://www.ai-cio.com/channel/GENERAL_SURVEYS/Moody_s_Says_Pension_Holes_May_Hurt_US_State_Ratings.html

9. Jeffrey, Terry, "Government Killed California," *Townhall.com* December 29, 2010.
http://townhall.com/columnists/TerryJeffrey/2010/12/29/government_killed_california

10. "Ducking Higher Taxes: Oregon's vanishing millionaires," *Wall Street Journal*, December 21, 2010.
http://online.wsj.com/article/SB10001424052748704034804576026233823935442.html

11. Malanga, Steven, "The 'Build America' Debt Bomb," *Wall Street Journal*, November 22, 2010.
http://online.wsj.com/article/SB10001424052748704648604575621062239887650.html?mod=googlenews_wsj

12. Barone, Michael, "For Tottering States, Bankruptcy Could Be the Answer," *Townhall.com*, November 29, 2010.
http://townhall.com/columnists/MichaelBarone/2010/11/29/for_tottering_states,_bankruptcy_could_be_the_answer

13. Bush, Jeb and Gingrich, Newt, "Better off bankrupt' *Los Angles Times*, January 27, 2011.
http://www.latimes.com/news/opinion/commentary/la-oe-gingrich-bankruptcy-20110127,0,4958969.story

14. Walsh, Mary Williams, "A Path Is Sought for States to Escape Their Debt Burdens," *New York Times*, January 20, 2011.
http://www.nytimes.com/2011/01/21/business/economy/21bankruptcy.html?_r=2&src=busln

15. McMahon, E. B., "State Bankruptcy Is a Bad Idea," *Wall Street Journal*, January 24, 2011.
http://online.wsj.com/article/SB10001424052748704881304576094091992 370356.html

16. Moya, Elena, "$2tn debt crisis threatens to bring down 100 US cities," *The Guardian*, December 20, 2010.
http://www.guardian.co.uk/business/2010/dec/20/debt-crisis-threatens-us-cities

17. de Rugy, Veronica, "The Municipal Debt Bubble," *Reason*, January, 2011.
http://reason.com/archives/2010/12/14/the-municipal-debt-bubble

18. Malange, Steven, "The Muni-Bond Debt Bond," *City Journal*, Summer, 2010.
http://www.city-journal.org/2010/20_3_muni-bonds.html

19. Grotto, James, "Politicians helped bring Chicago's public pension funds to the brink of insolvency," *Chicago Tribune*, November 16, 2010.
http://www.chicagotribune.com/news/local/ct-met-pensions-deals-20101116,0,4059864.story

20. Grotto, James, "Tribune Watchdog: Pension bets not paying off," *Chicago Tribune*, November 17, 2010.
http://archive.chicagobreakingnews.com/2010/11/tribune-watchdog-pension-bets-not-paying-off.html

21. "The Suicide Pacts," *Chicago Tribune*, November 27, 2010.
http://articles.chicagotribune.com/2010-11-27/news/ct-edit-pension-20101127_1_suicide-pacts-retirement-deals-unions

22. Secter, Bob, "Chicago taxpayers on hook for 444 percent more in government pensions than decade ago, report says" *Chicago Tribune*.
http://newsblogs.chicagotribune.com/clout_st/2010/03/chicago-taxpayers-on-hook-for-444-percent-more-in-government-pensions-than-a-decade-ago-report-says.html

23. Wessel, David, "What Sent States' Fiscal Picture Into a Tailspin?" *Wall Street Journal*, January 27, 2011.
http://online.wsj.com/article/SB10001424052748704062604576105912876030294.html

24. "Examiner Editorial: Time to get real about public-sector pensions," *Washington Examiner*, January 25, 2011.
http://washingtonexaminer.com/opinion/editorials/2011/01/examiner-editorial-time-get-real-about-public-sector-pensions

25. Byrne, Dennis, "The worst is yet to come in Illinois," Chicago Tribune, January 25, 2011.
http://www.chicagotribune.com/news/opinion/ct-oped-0125-byrne-20110125,0,1807309.column

26. Chambers, Jennifer, "Without aid, DPS may close half of its schools" *Detroit News*, January 12, 2011.
http://detnews.com/article/20110112/SCHOOLS/101120356/Without-aid--DPS-may-close-half-of-its-schools

27. Thompson, Krissah, "With Detroit in dire straits, mayor invites big thinking," *Washington Post*, February 8, 2011.
http://www.washingtonpost.com/wp-dyn/content/article/2011/02/07/AR2011020705338.html?wpisrc=nl_pmheadline

28. Stevens, Elizabeth Lesly, "Bonus Payments to City Retirees Are Drawing Ire," *New York Times*, January 20, 2011.
http://www.nytimes.com/2011/01/21/us/21bccola.html?_r=3

29. Goldman, Harry, "New York City Budget Deficit Next Year May Widen by $2 Billion, Page Says," *Bloomberg*, December 6, 2011.
http://www.bloomberg.com/news/2010-12-06/new-york-city-budget-gap-may-widen-by-2-billion-next-year-official-says.html

30. Bush, Rudolph, "Dallas City Hall could face another massive budget deficit for 2011-12," *Dallas Morning News*, January 18, 2011
http://www.dallasnews.com/news/community-news/dallas/headlines/20110118-dallas-city-hall-could-face-another-massive-budget-deficit-for-2011-12.ece

31. Laksin, Jacob, "Poverty-ridden Camden, N.J., faces police cuts amid increasing crime," *The Washington Examiner*, February 8, 2011.
http://washingtonexaminer.com/opinion/columnists/2011/02/manhattan-moment-poverty-ridden-camden-nj-faces-police-cuts-amid-increasi

32. Evans, Donald, "Hidden Pension Fiasco May Foment Another $1 Trillion Bailout," *Bloomberg,* March 3, 2009.
http://www.bloomberg.com/apps/news?pid=newsarchive&sid=alwTE0Z5.1EA

33. Hughes, Brian, "Salaries of local government brass top Biden's, Cabinet secretaries'," *Washington Examiner*, December 27, 2010.
http://washingtonexaminer.com/local/dc/2010/12/top-local-government-brass-rake-big-bucks

34. Cauchon, Dennis, "More federal workers' pay tops $150,000," *USA Today*, November 10, 2010.
http://www.usatoday.com/news/nation/2010-11-10-1Afedpay10_ST_N.htm

35. Rein, Lisa, "Federal workers campaign against proposed cuts," *Washington Post*, February 9, 2011.
http://www.washingtonpost.com/wp-dyn/content/article/2011/02/09/AR2011020906742.html?wpisrc=nl_pmheadline

Chapter Three: Destroying America through immigration

1. "Hispanic Americans by the Numbers," *U.S. Census Bureau.*
http://www.infoplease.com/spot/hhmcensus1.html

2. Bartlett, Bruce, "Poverty Yardstick Notes," *The Washington Times*, October 5, 2003.
http://www.washingtontimes.com/news/2003/oct/5/20031005-111129-3478r/

3. "Unauthorized Immigrant Population: National and State Trends, 2010" *Pew Hispanic Center*, February 1, 2011
http://pewhispanic.org/files/reports/133.pdf

4. Sowell, Thomas, "Red Herring politics, Part II," *TownHall*, October 6, 2010.
http://townhall.com/columnists/ThomasSowell/2010/10/06/red_herring_politics_part_ii/page/1

5. Rector, Robert, "Importing Poverty: Immigration and Poverty in the United States: A Book of Charts," *The Heritage Foundation*, October 26, 2006.
http://www.heritage.org/Research/Reports/2006/10/Importing-Poverty-Immigration-and-Poverty-in-the-United-States-A-Book-of-Charts

6. "Breaking the Piggy Bank: How Illegal Immigration is Sending Schools Into the Red," *Federation for American Immigration Reform*, June 2005.
http://www.mnforsustain.org/immg_costs_of_educating_legal_illegals_fair.htm

7. Rubenstein, Ruben, "Criminal Alien Nation," *Vdare.com*, June 30, 2005.
http://www.vdare.com/rubenstein/050630_nd.htm

8. Krutzman, Joel, "Mexico's Instability Is a Real Problem," *Wall Street Journal*, January 16, 2009.
http://online.wsj.com/article/SB123206674721488169.html

9. "Immigration and Welfare," *Federation for American Immigration Reform*, June, 2010.
http://www.fairus.org/site/News2?page=NewsArticle&id=16985&security=16 01&news_iv_ctrl=1017#end

10. "The High Cost of Cheap Labor: Illegal Immigration and the Federal Budget," *Center for Immigration Studies*, 2002 numbers.
http://cis.org/articles/2004/fiscalexec.html

11. McCombs, Brady, "Barriers aren't just for the border now" *Arizona Daily Star*, January 25, 2011.
http://azstarnet.com/news/local/border/article_e1986b5f-ab07-5d81-9249-326ca0da28a6.html

12. Dvorek, Kimberly, "Anchor babies cost Los Angeles welfare $600 million last year," *San Diego County Political Buzz Examiner*, January 20, 2011
http://www.examiner.com/county-political-buzz-in-san-diego/anchor-babies-cost-los-angeles-welfare-600-million-last-year#ixzz1BatAfaA0

13. "Immigration Front: Violence in Juárez Eclipses That in Afghanistan," *The Patriot Post*, March 4, 2011.
http://patriotpost.us/edition/2011/03/04/digest/

14. Shirk, Roland, "Trust by E-verify," *Jihad Watch*, February 9, 2011.
http://www.jihadwatch.org/2011/02/trust-but-e-verify.html

15. Nowrasteh, Alex, "Keeping Out Foreign Workers Is Crushing America's Growth," *Investor's Business Daily*, February, 16 2011.
http://www.investors.com/NewsAndAnalysis/Article/563375/201102161754/Keeping-Out-Foreign-Workers-Is-Crushing-Americas-Growth.aspx

16. Steyn, Mark, "Fortress Europe," *Steyn Online*, February 9, 2011.
http://www.steynonline.com/content/view/3704/

17. Duke, Selwyn, "The Brit PM's Limp Attack on Multiculturalism," *American Thinker*, February 6, 2011.
http://www.americanthinker.com/blog/2011/02/the_brit_pms_limp_attack_on_mu.html

Chapter Four: The Twin Jihads—Working in Tandem to Wreck the Republic

1. "Islamophobia," *Wikipedia.*
http://en.wikipedia.org/wiki/Islamophobia

2. "List of Islamic Attacks Against America...before 9/11," *Fact Real*, January 30, 2010.
http://factreal.wordpress.com/2010/01/30/list-of-islamic-attacks-against-america/

3. Kasar, Veysel, *Questions on Islam,* December 2010.
http://www.questionsonislam.com/index.php?s=show_qna&id=3129

4. *Islamization Watch*, December 6, 2010.
http://islamizationwatch.blogspot.com/2010/12/turkeys-power-hungry-islamist-pm.html

5. "Islamic flag over the White House," *Washington Times*, October 4, 2010.
http://www.washingtontimes.com/news/2010/oct/4/islamic-flag-over-the-white-house/

6. "Extremism and the Council on American-Islamic Relations (CAIR)" *Citizens United*, January, 2007
http://www.scribd.com/doc/50301189/59/Organizational-Links-to-Hamas-Infrastructure

7. "America Exposed to 'Stealth Jihad' Threat, Security Report Warns" *Fox News*, September 15, 2010.
http://www.foxnews.com/politics/2010/09/15/america-threatened-stealth-jihad-security-report-warns/

8. Spencer, Robert, *Stealth Jihad: How Radical Islam is Subverting America without Guns or Bombs,* 2008.
http://www.amazon.com/Stealth-Jihad-Radical-Subverting-America/dp/1596985569

9. "The Islamic Demolition of the Statue of Liberty," *Shariah4America.com.*
http://shariah4america.com/NewYork/The-Islamic-Demolition-of-the-Statue-of-Liberty

10. "Airport adds foot basins for Muslim cabbies," *World Net Daily*, April 28, 2007.
http://www.wnd.com/news/article.asp?ARTICLE_ID=55417

11. Lewin, Terry, "Some U.S. universities install foot baths for Muslim students" *New York Times,* August 7, 2011.
http://www.nytimes.com/2007/08/07/world/americas/07iht-muslims.4.7022566.html

12. "Mich. City Council OKs Muslim Prayer Over Loudspeaker," *Associated Press*, April 20, 2004.
http://www.foxnews.com/story/0,2933,117705,00.html

13. Pinto, Barbara, "Muslim Cab Drivers Refuse to Transport Alcohol, and Dogs," *ABC News*, Jan. 26, 2007
http://abcnews.go.com/International/story?id=2827800&page=1

14. Unruh, Bob, "'Five pillars of Islam' taught in public school," *World Net Daily*, October 10, 2006.
http://www.wnd.com/?pageId=38269

15. "Uswa Hasana," *WikiIslam*
http://wikiislam.net/wiki/Uswa_Hasana

16. "Translation of Sahih Bukhari, Book 62," *University of Southern California, Center for Muslim-Jewish Engagement.*
http://www.usc.edu/schools/college/crcc/engagement/resources/texts/muslim/hadith/bukhari/062.sbt.html

17. "Child Sex OK at Age 9, says Islamic Saudi Cleric," *World Net Daily*, June 27, 2008.
http://www.wnd.com/index.php?fa=PAGE.view&pageId=68074

18. "Islam and slavery," *Wikipedia.*
http://en.wikipedia.org/wiki/Islam_and_slavery

19. "Slavery is a part of Islam," *Crethi Plethi*, May 8, 2010.
http://www.crethiplethi.com/slavery-is-a-part-of-islam/global-islam/2010/

20. "Slavery in Sudan," *Gates of Vienna.*
http://gatesofvienna.blogspot.com/2011/03/slavery-in-sudan.html

21. "Women's Rights and the Sharia," *Islam and Modernity.*
http://www.ntpi.org/html/womensrights.html

22. "How Sharia Law Punishes Raped Women," *Assyrian International News Agency*, November 17, 2008.
http://www.aina.org/news/20081117111817.htm

23. Hughes, Mark and Taylor, Jerome, "Rape 'impossible' in marriage, says Muslim cleric," *The Independent*, October 14, 2010.
http://www.independent.co.uk/news/uk/home-news/rape-impossible-in-marriage-says-muslim-cleric-2106161.html

24. "Islamic Law," *WikiIslam*.
http://wikiislam.net/wiki/Islamic_law

25. "Questions about Apostasy (Blasphemy)" *Al-Sunna.org, Islamic Studies*.
http://www.webcitation.org/query?url=http://www.alsunna.org/Questions-about-Apostasy-Blasphemy.html&date=2011-02-25

26. "Pakistani Christian Sentenced for 'Blasphemy' Dies in Prison," *Compass Direct News*, March 15, 2011.
http://www.compassdirect.org/english/country/pakistan/98521/

27. Sen, Ashish Kumar, "Pakistan minister murdered for criticism of Islam blasphemy law," *Washington Times*, March 2, 2011`.
http://www.washingtontimes.com/news/2011/mar/2/pakistan-minister-murdered-for-criticism-of-islam-/

28. Dogar, Babar, "Pakistan governor's suspected assassin hailed as hero," *Washington Times*, January 5, 2011.
http://www.washingtontimes.com/news/2011/jan/5/pakistani-governor-buried-under-tightened-security/

29. Davis, Gregory M., "Islam 101"
http://www.jihadwatch.org/islam-101.html

30. "Egypt: Christians call for repeal of dhimmi law restricting church construction," *Jihad Watch*, January 22, 2011.
http://www.jihadwatch.org/2011/01/egypt-christians-call-for-repeal-of-dhimmi-law-restricting-church-construction.html

31. "Muslim leaders agree, death penalty for gays (video)" *Creeping Sharia*, February 13, 2010.
http://creepingsharia.wordpress.com/2010/02/13/muslim-leaders-agree-death-for-gays/

32. "Eurabia," *Wikipedia*.
http://en.wikipedia.org/wiki/Eurabia

33. Meo, Nick, "Jews leave Swedish city after sharp rise in anti-Semitic hate crimes," *The Telegraph*, February 21, 2010.
http://www.telegraph.co.uk/news/worldnews/europe/sweden/7278532/Jews-leave-Swedish-city-after-sharp-rise-in-anti-Semitic-hate-crimes.html

34. Pipes, Daniel, "The 751 No-Go Zones of France," *DanielPipes.org*, January 16, 2010.
http://www.danielpipes.org/blog/2006/11/the-751-no-go-zones-of-france

35. Lapkin, Sharon, "Western Muslims' Racist Rape Spree," *FrontPageMag.com*, December 29, 2005.
http://www.rense.com/general69/westernmuslims.htm

36. Bellil, Samira, "The Hell of the Tournantes," *Wikipedia*.
http://en.wikipedia.org/wiki/Samira_Bellil

37. "Elisabeth's Voice: The Archives," *Gates of Vienna*, February 21, 2011.
http://gatesofvienna.blogspot.com/2011/02/elisabeths-voice-archives.html

38. Hayes, Patrick, "First They Came For The Faux Fascists," *Spiked*, March 14, 2011.
http://www.spiked-online.com/index.php/site/article/10290/

39. Steyn, Mark, "Lars man standing – again," *Steyn Online*, January 25, 2011.
http://www.steynonline.com/content/view/3661/128/

40. Steyn, Mark, "The absurd trial of Geert Wilders," *Macleans.ca*, January 25, 2010.
http://www.steynonline.com/content/view/3661/128/

41. Landen, Thomas, "Dutch Police Arrests Cartoonist," *The Brussels Journal*, May 16, 2008.
http://www.brusselsjournal.com/node/3257

42. Webster, Paul, "Calling Islam stupid lands author in court," *The Guardian*, September 18, 2002.
http://www.guardian.co.uk/world/2002/sep/18/booksnews.islam

43. Steyn, Mark, "The Steynonline Free Speech Special" *Steyn Online*, 2011.
(Note: this is an offering of books about the cases.)
http://www.steynstore.com/product66.html

44. Steyn, Mark, **"Fortress Europe?"** *Steyn online,* February 9, 2011
http://www.steynonline.com/content/view/3704/

45. "A Stranger in My Own Land," *Standpoint*, January/February, 2011, http://www.standpointmag.co.uk/node/3650/full

46. "Fall of Constantinople," *Wikipedia*.
http://en.wikipedia.org/wiki/Fall_of_Constantinople

47. Navarro, Peter and Spencer, Aron, "September 11 2001 Assessing the Costs of Terrorism. *Milken Institute Review*, Fourth Quarter, 2001
http://www.milkeninstitute.org/publications/review/2001_12/16-31mr.pdf

48. Tapson, Mark, "Apocalypse Imminent," Pajamas Media, February 13, 2011.
"http://pajamasmedia.com/blog/apocalypse-imminent/?singlepage=true

49. "US Muslim TV boss 'beheaded wife,'" *BBC News*, February 17, 2009.
http://news.bbc.co.uk/2/hi/7894721.stm

50. Miklaszewski, Jim, "9 officers face disciplinary action in Fort Hood shooting," *MSNBC*, March 10, 2011.
http://www.msnbc.msn.com/id/42017230/ns/us_news-security/

51. "Muslim Publics Divided on Hamas and Hezbollah," *Pew Global Attitudes Project*, December 2, 2010.
http://pewglobal.org/2010/12/02/muslims-around-the-world-divided-on-hamas-and-hezbollah/

52. Kerwick, Jack, "Islam Perceived versus Islam Itself," *The Patriot Post*, March 15, 2011.
http://patriotpost.us/commentary/2011/03/15/islam-perceived-versus-islam-itself/

53. "Why Sharia Law must be opposed," *No To Political Islam*
http://www.ntpi.org/html/whyoppose.html

54. Shoebat, Walid, "Terrorism hearing testimony in absentia," *The Right Scoop*, March 22, 2011.
http://www.therightscoop.com/walid-shoebat-terrorism-hearing-testimony-in-absentia/

55. Kessler, Oren, "'Democracy and political Islam can't coexist,'" *The Jerusalem Post*, March 18, 2011.
http://www.jpost.com/International/Article.aspx?id=212706

56. Nomani, Asra, "Profile Me, Please! King's Muslim Hearings Are No Witch Hunt," *The Daily Beast*, March 7, 2011.
http://www.thedailybeast.com/blogs-and-stories/2011-03-07/peter-kings-hearings-on-american-muslims-are-no-witch-hunt/

57. Mahmud, Hasan, "To Stop or Not to Stop Sharia," *Front Page Magazine*, November 3, 2010.
http://frontpagemag.com/2010/11/03/to-stop-or-not-to-stop-sharia/print/

58. Hamid, Tawfik, "From the heart of a Muslim," *CPlash*, April 20, 2010.
http://cplash.com/post/From-the-heart-of-a-Muslim---Tawfik-Hamid901.html

59. May, Carolyn, "Ahmadiyya Muslim Community Launches 'Muslims for Loyalty' Campaign," *The Daily Caller*, February 5, 2011.
http://dailycaller.com/2011/02/05/muslims-loyalty/

60. Women Against Sharia
http://womenagainstshariah.blogspot.com/

61. Muslims Against Sharia
http://muslimsagainstsharia.blogspot.com/

62. Muslims for Progressive Values
http://www.mpvusa.org/

63. Munro, Neil, "White House to liberal-minded Muslims: Drop Dead." *The Daily Caller*, March 9, 2011.
http://dailycaller.com/2011/03/09/white-house-to-liberal-minded-muslims-drop-dead/

64. "Outspoken Muslim cleric killed in northern Nigeria," *AFP*, March 13, 2011.
http://www.google.com/hostednews/afp/article/ALeqM5i7lXDsVHDzZO3ZNeUw_xsd5KaD8Q?docId=CNG.c105341bf1df5116fb348c673eb9322d.13e1

65. "Bomb wounds four at Indonesian Islam group HQ" *AFP*, March 15, 2011.
http://www.google.com/hostednews/afp/article/ALeqM5hoXm56iYPH9m9T_8pfkDvKQevqpQ?docId=CNG.109ca1c1340ce42e33e6f0390a02cf2c.e1

66. *Infidel* by Ayaan Hirsi Ali
http://www.amazon.com/Infidel-Ayaan-Hirsi-Ali/dp/0743289684

67. "Muslims speak out against terrorism," *God's Eye View*, October 25, 2006.
http://revjimsutter.blogspot.com/2006/10/muslims-speak-out-against-terrorism.html

68. "Deadly Terror Attacks since 9/11," *The Religion of Peace*
http://www.thereligionofpeace.com/

69. Moran, Rick, "West Bank family murdered in their sleep: Palestinians celebrate," *American Thinker*, March 12, 2011.
http://www.americanthinker.com/blog/2011/03/west_bank_family_murdered_in_t.html
Photos of the Murdered Children:
https://picasaweb.google.com/picsyesha/Itamar

70. Rusin, David J., "Violent Jihad Kills Muslims, 'Islamophobia' Does Not," *Islamist Watch*, March 25, 2011.
http://www.islamist-watch.org/blog/2011/03/violent-jihad-kills-muslims-islamophobia-does-not

71. "Battle of Tours, 732," *Web Chronology Project*
http://www.thenagain.info/webchron/westeurope/tours.html

72. "Siege of Vienna, 1529," *Wikipedia*
http://en.wikipedia.org/wiki/Siege_of_Vienna

73. "Jan III Sobieski: 1674-1696 And The Siege of Vienna of 1683," *Web Chronology Project*
http://www.thenagain.info/webchron/EastEurope/ViennaSiege.html

74. Hanson, Victor Davis, "Don John of Austria Is Riding to the Sea," July 12, 2007.
http://www.victorhanson.com/articles/hanson071207.html

Chapter Five: China—Does the Dragon Awake?

1. "Market Reforms for China," *Cato Institute*, October 1997
http://www.cato.org/pubs/policy_report/cpr-19n5-5.html

2. "Mandate of Heaven," *Wikipedia*.
http://en.wikipedia.org/wiki/Mandate_of_Heaven

3. "Foreign relations of Imperial China," *Wikipedia*.
http://en.wikipedia.org/wiki/Foreign_relations_of_Imperial_China

4. Yihong, Pan, "Traditional Chinese Theories of Foreign Relations and Tang Foreign Policy," *North American-China Research Project*, 1998.
http://www.cic.sfu.ca/nacrp/articles/panyihong/panyihongtext.html

5. "The Guomindang (Kuomintang), the Nationalist Party of China," *San José State University Department of Economics*.
http://www.applet-magic.com/guomindang.htm

6. "Chronology of the Tibetan Resistance Movement," *Tibet Sites*, April 30, 2010.
http://www.tibetsites.com/articles/Chronology-of-the-Tibetan-Resistance-Movement-a9.html

7. "US and Vietnam demonstrate blossoming military relationship," *The Telegraph*, August 8, 2010.
http://www.telegraph.co.uk/news/worldnews/asia/vietnam/7933666/US-and-Vietnam-demonstrate-blossoming-military-relationship.html

8. Morris, Ian, "The next 40 years will be the most important in human history," *Jewish World Review*, December 10, 2010.
http://www.jewishworldreview.com/1210/next_40_years.php3

9. Helprin, Mark, "The Decline of U.S. Naval Power," *Wall Street Journal*, March 2, 2011.
http://online.wsj.com/article/SB1000142405274870415060457616636251295 2294.html

10. Will, George, "Thinking like a master," *The Patriot Post*, March 20, 2011.
http://patriotpost.us/opinion/george-will/2011/03/20/thinking-like-a-master/

11. Kudlow, Larry, "How to combat an arrogant China," *Townhall Finance*, January 20, 2011
http://finance.townhall.com/columnists/larrykudlow/2011/01/20/how_to_combat_an_arrogant_china

12. Dalanian, Ken, "China's development of stealth fighter takes U.S. by surprise," *Los Angles Times*, January 7, 2011.
http://www.latimes.com/news/nationworld/world/la-fg-china-military-20110107,0,3324067.story?om_rid=Mqh-Do&om_mid=_BNJxIvB8XEExMK

13. Blanc, Sebastien, "Aircraft carrier plan shows China naval ambitions," *AFP*, November 17, 2010.
http://www.google.com/hostednews/afp/article/ALeqM5ihRKU61Wyeg-pZin9lLTdRpIZ-2w?docId=CNG.281e53569e8cb9a89178810c1be014e6.231

14. Moran, Rick, "What, me worry? China ups defense spending 12.7%," *American Thinker*, March 4, 2011.
http://www.americanthinker.com/blog/2011/03/what_me_worry_china_ups_defens.html

15. Carafano, James, "Obama needs to address our cyber-warfare gap with China," *Washington Examiner*, January 23, 2011.
http://washingtonexaminer.com/opinion/columnists/2011/01/obama-needs-address-our-cyber-warfare-gap-china

16. Ignatius, David, "Warfare of the Future," *Real Clear Politics*, January 2, 2011.
http://www.realclearpolitics.com/articles/2011/01/02/warfare_of_the_future_108407.html

17. "China overtakes Japan as world's second-biggest economy," *BBC News*, 14 February 2011.
http://www.bbc.co.uk/news/business-12427321

18. Taylor, James M., "New EPA Data Show Futility Of U.S. Carbon Dioxide Restrictions." *Forbes*, February 24, 2011.
http://www.forbes.com/2011/02/23/china-carbon-dioxide-emissions-opinions-contributors-james-taylor.html

19. Noonan, Sean, "Chinese Espionage and French Trade Secrets," *StratFor*, January 20, 2011.
http://www.stratfor.com/weekly/20110119-chinese-espionage-and-french-trade-secrets?utm_source=SWeekly&utm_medium=e-mail&utm_campaign=110120&utm_content=readmore&elq=3380ea4bd4124f619ad734b308bc3fde

20. Watts, Anthony, "China announces thorium reactor energy program, Obama still dwelling on 'Sputnik moments,'" *What's Up With That*, January 30, 2011.
http://wattsupwiththat.com/2011/01/30/china-announces-thorium-reactor-energy-program-obama-still-dwelling-on-sputnik-moments/#more-32829

21. Das, Anil, "Facts of China's rare earth reserves," *International Business Times*, March 3, 2011.
http://uk.ibtimes.com/articles/118284/20110303/rare-earth-minerals-china-u-s-geological-survey.htm

22. Staley, Stanley, "China, High Speed Rail, and Mobility," *Reason Foundation*, January 13, 2011.
http://reason.org/blog/show/china-high-speed-rail-and-mobility

23. Summers, Graham, "China's Fires the Warning Shot on US Debt," *Phoenix Capital Research*, January, 2011
http://www.zerohedge.com/article/china's-fires-warning-shot-us-debt?utm_source=feedburner&utm_medium=feed&utm_campaign=Feed%3A+zerohedge%2Ffeed+%28zero+hedge+-+on+a+long+enough+timeline%2C+the+survival+rate+for+everyone+drops+to+zero%29

24. Griswold, Daniel, "Deal with the Dragon," *National Review*, March 31, 2011.
http://www.cato.org/pub_display.php?pub_id=12900

25. Carafano, James Jay, "Ignoring Chinas military buildup at our own peril," *Washington Examiner*, January 30, 2011.
http://washingtonexaminer.com/opinion/columnists/2011/01/ignoring-chinas-military-buildup-our-own-peril

26, Goldberg, Jonah, "Americas China Syndrome," *The Patriot Post*, January 19, 2011.
http://patriotpost.us/opinion/jonah-goldberg/2011/01/19/americas-china-syndrome/

27. "Pollution a threat to China's growth, " *UPI.com*, March 1, 2011.
http://www.upi.com/Science_News/Resource-Wars/2011/03/01/Pollution-a-threat-to-Chinas-growth/UPI-94781299004853/

28. Hitchens, Peter, "China Gendercide: China's shameful massacre of unborn girls means there will soon be 30m more men than women," *Mail Online.com*, April 10, 2010.
http://www.newser.com/story/85816/china-faces-a-future-with-too-many-men.html

29. Schiff, Peter, "China's Inflation Problem Looms Large," *Common American Journal*, January 19, 2011.
http://commonamericanjournal.com/?p=24000

30. Solomon, Lawrence, "China's Coming fall," *National Post*, January 22, 2011.
http://fullcomment.nationalpost.com/2011/01/22/lawrence-solomon-china%E2%80%99s-fall/

Chapter Six: What Will a Collapse Look Like?

1. Kratman, Tom, *Caliphate,* Baen Books, April, 2008.
http://www.amazon.com/Caliphate-Tom-Kratman/dp/1439133425/ref=sr_1_9?s=books&ie=UTF8&qid=1301675143&sr=1-9

2. "Hyperinflation in Zimbabwe," *Wikipedia*.
http://en.wikipedia.org/wiki/Hyperinflation_in_Zimbabwe

3. "Argentina Inflation Rate," *Trading Economics*
http://www.tradingeconomics.com/Economics/Inflation-CPI.
aspx?Symbol=ARS

4. "Report: 230,000 Displaced By Mexico's Drug War," *Associated Press*, April 1, 2011.
http://www.npr.org/templates/story/story.php?storyId=103181125

5. Obome, Peter, "Some European countries are in the habit of going bankrupt," *The Telegraph*, March 24, 2011.
http://blogs.telegraph.co.uk/news/peteroborne/100081316/some-european-countries-are-in-the-habit-of-going-bankrupt/

6. Dilanian, Ken, "Virtual war a real threat," *Las Angles Times*, March 28, 2011.
http://articles.latimes.com/2011/mar/28/nation/la-na-cyber-war-20110328

7. Hall, Robert A., "A Bit of Colored Ribbon," *Another Realm*, 1999.
http://www.anotherealm.com/1999/flash/ribbon.html

8. Dickson, Gordon R., *Wolf and Iron*, Tom Doherty Associates, 1990.
http://www.amazon.com/Wolf-Iron-Gordon-R-Dickson/dp/0812533348/ref=sr_1_1?s=books&ie=UTF8&qid=1301805315&sr=1-1

Chapter Seven: How Did We Get in This Mess?

1. Sowell, Thomas, "Another Great Depressions?" *Creators.com*, 2008
http://www.creators.com/opinion/thomas-sowell/another-great-depression.html

2. Indiviglio, Daniel, "Is the U.S. Becoming a Welfare State?" *The Atlantic*, March 9, 2011.
http://www.theatlantic.com/business/archive/2011/03/is-the-us-becoming-a-welfare-state/72217/

3. "How Many Trillions Must We Waste on the War on Poverty?" *Heritage Foundation*, March 17, 2011.
http://blog.heritage.org/2011/03/17/morning-bell-how-many-trillions-must-we-waste-on-the-war-on-poverty/?

4. Hymowittz, Kay, " Breakdown Of The Black Family, And Its Consequences," *DiscovertheNetworks.org*, August 25, 2005.
http://www.discoverthenetworks.org/viewSubCategory.asp?id=1261

5. Sahadi, Jeanne, "47% will pay no federal income tax," *CNN Money*, October 3, 2009.
http://money.cnn.com/2009/09/30/pf/taxes/who_pays_taxes/index.htm

6. Hollingsworth, Babara, "Majority of American students flunk civics test," *The Washington Examiner*, March 5, 2011.
http://washingtonexaminer.com/blogs/beltway-confidential/2011/03/majority-american-students-flunk-civics-test

7. "Grim Illiteracy Statistics Indicate Americans Have a Reading Problem," *EducationPortal.com*, September 20, 2007.
http://education-portal.com/articles/Grim_Illiteracy_Statistics_Indicate_Americans_Have_a_Reading_Problem.html

8. "Most Americans Can't Name Any Supreme Court Justices," *AOL News*, Jun 2, 2010
http://www.aolnews.com/2010/06/02/most-americans-cant-name-any-supreme-court-justices/

9. Lubold, Gordon, "Will Ivy League embrace R.O.T.C again?" *Christian Science Monitor*, September 19, 2008
http://www.csmonitor.com/USA/Military/2008/0919/p02s02-usmi.html

Chapter Eight: What Can You Do to Prevent a Collapse?

1. "Orc," *Wikipedia*
http://en.wikipedia.org/wiki/Orc

2. Krauthammer, Charles, "Obama's Social Security Hoax," *The Patriot Post*, March 11, 2011.
http://patriotpost.us/opinion/charles-krauthammer/2011/03/11/obamas-social-security-hoax/

3. "Fix the Primaries."
http://fixtheprimaries.com/solutions/americanplan/

4. Ayn Rand Lexicon
http://aynrandlexicon.com/lexicon/compromise.html

5. "A Report on the Litigation Lobby, 2010," *Trial Lawyers Inc.: K Street*
http://www.triallawyersinc.com/kstreet/kstr01.html

Conclusion

1. Goldfarb, Zachary A. and Montgomery, Lori, "S&P lowers its outlook on U.S. debt; stocks decline," *Washington Post*, April 18, 2011.
http://www.washingtonpost.com/business/economy/sandp-lowers-its-outlook-on-us-debt-stocks-decline/2011/04/18/AFRK601D_story.html?nl_headlines

Made in the USA
Lexington, KY
08 July 2011